The Forgetting Tree

The Forgetting Tree

A Rememory

Rae Paris

Wayne State University Press
Detroit

ISBN 978-0-8143-4426-2 (paperback); ISBN 978-0-8143-4427-9 (ebook)
Library of Congress Cataloging Number: 2017953474

Published with support from the Arthur L. Johnson Fund for African American Studies.

Wayne State University Press
Leonard N. Simons Building
4809 Woodward Avenue
Detroit, Michigan 48201-1309

Visit us online at wsupress.wayne.edu

for Daddy
and
for the others
of us
in and on
the ground

To recall you all

demands the voice and memory

of brief madness beyond pain.

—Kofi Awoonor

But it's freedom or death, exert speed till my last breath

—Brand Nubian

Contents

IV. Sinew

V. Souls

Postlude 143

Give Thanks 144

Notes 147

Acknowledgments

Some of these poems (and previous versions) first saw the light of day through the generous work of the editors and staff at the following publications. Many thanks.

*Killens Review of Arts and Letters; Cosmonauts Avenue; Women: A Cultural Review; The Offing; Tor House Foundation; Transition Magazine: The Magazine of Africa and the Diaspora; The Common; Hobart Pulp: Another Literary Journal; Solstice: A Magazine of Diverse Voices; Guernica: A Magazine of Art & Politic*s, *What Matters,* edited by Richard Krawiek, and *The Mighty Stream: Poems in Celebration of Martin Luther King,* edited by Carolyn Forché and Jackie Kay.

"Uncle Kwanza: November 1," also appeared in *Coiled Serpent: Poets Arising from the Cultural Quakes and Shifts in Los Angeles,* edited by Daniel A. Olivas, Neelanjana Banerjee, Ruben J. Rodriguez.

"Strangled: Letter to a Young Black Poet," also appeared in *Resisting Arrest: Poems to Stretch the Sky,* edited by Tony Medina.

"The Hanging Tree" also appeared in *SolLit Selects: Diverse Voices.*

"The Forgetting Tree" also appeared in *Best of the Net 2013 Anthology.*

Deep gratitude as well to the following institutions, organizations, and foundations, which provided time, space, and funding: Michigan State University, Hedgebrook, the Helene Wurlitzer Foundation, Hambidge, Atlantic Center for the Arts, and the National Endowment for the Arts.

Prelude
Office of the Dead

thinking of Boston after the bombing,
and Pablo Neruda

Dig up the bones all the bones the severed
legs mourning knee fallen lash blistered air,
hallowed eyes in faces torn the weathered
men and women low prostrate hands in hair.
Dig up lost thumb split nail ring ruined hand,
tongue and teeth and shoe and skin blood-stained sole
of feet. Tear up the sidewalk, glass and sand,
and open mouth and ear each ruptured hole,
inside somewhere the poison lives. Let's check
latticework of tissue bone all the plates
and cells. Let's lace this grieving spring night speck
of sky. Dig up today, what fate awaits?
Beware the dark-skinned men says faithful cop.
A limbless boy just eight should make us stop.

1. Bones

we are the bones
of what you forget

—Wendy Rose

How I Write: On Forgetting

Questions that might get closer to the truth: At what point in time do I write? At what point in place and space?

Let me tell you about my complicated research methods:

1. Look at a map the day before you drive and see what cities you'll pass through.
2. Google the city, along with "segregation," "plantation," "lynching." Also google "Black people," or "African Americans" and "Rebellion."
3. You'll always find something.

Summer 2010

I take a solo drive across the country—Tempe, Arizona to Ripton, Vermont via New Orleans. On my way to one of the Whitest states in the union to meet my husband who's working for the first time at what I'll eventually start referring to as The Whitest School of English. My plan is to stop at plantations and other sites of terror, as well as sites of resistance. My last stop before Vermont will be Auburn, New York to visit Harriet Tubman's resting place. I'm in the middle of a NEA Literature Fellowship and this drive is part of my research. I'm thinking it might inform a future collection of stories, possibly set in New Orleans and other parts of the South, or maybe some essays. I'm interested in the ways we preserve the past, we mostly being, but not limited to, the settler colonial nation state most commonly referred to as the United States. I'm interested in what we build monuments to, the fictions we tell about our not-so-distant, troubled yesterday, and how these fictions inform and shape our violent present.

I'm not quite sure what I'm doing.

I'm guilty of romanticizing the South to a certain extent—as much as any first generation Great Migration Black woman might let Black girl desire for back home and Black home romanticize a place they've never actually lived for any significant amount of time, and have constructed mostly from other people's shaky, loving dreams; joy-filled lies; and hard felt terror, but I do romanticize it, especially New Orleans.

When my parents left New Orleans in the late fifties and moved to southern California, first to L.A. and then just outside of L.A., about a half hour south of downtown, to our red-lined Black neighborhood where most if not all of the families were from somewhere South—Louisiana, Mississippi, Alabama—they, of course, brought their stories with them. Of course, they probably talked about New Orleans more than I remember, but, as I say again and again, it's the silence that sticks with me, always at the edges and underneath their stories about what it meant for my parents to come of age under segregation, to be poor, to be the first ones in their families to attend and graduate from college, what it meant to leave their families, what it meant for my father to be one of the few Black people working at the IRS. I can hear my mother as I write this: *Stop it. Quit being so melodramatic. Everybody was poor back then.*

Once, in a phone conversation when I was in college, I asked my father about his parents and grandparents. He might've asked me why I wanted to know, and because I was at a stage where I was taking Black history and literature classes for the first time and thought I knew more in some ways than my parents, I might've said something about how important it was for me to know the history of our family so I could know who I was, and because my father had a sense of humor he might've said something funny and sarcastic about how could I *not* know who I was and did I need him to tell me who I was and was I just wasting time up there at that school where he was sending me money, but I wouldn't let up. At the time, I wasn't thinking enough about what it might mean for my parents to talk about their past, what it might mean for them to speak it to their children or anyone, but especially to their children who they loved and who they may have wanted to offer themselves to as whole and not hurt, to their children who they wanted to live free, free-er than they had been able to live, and free to them maybe meant putting away certain pieces of a past, locking it all up and moving on as well as one could. And, of course, this isn't in absence of Black joy, but I wasn't thinking enough about the trauma and sometime sadness of not only living Black life but of telling it. *This is not a story to pass on.*

When my father could hear I wasn't going to let him be, he may have sighed. I can maybe hear him sighing even now, and then he said, "Well you know about . . . ," and he told me about his grandfather on his father's side, the one nobody knew was White until he, my great-grandfather, died, and that side of the family came to the funeral. No, I didn't know about this, had never heard this sliver of story that held so much and my father telling me in his calm, bored, lecture voice like it was something he had shared thousands of times and here I was making him say it again and for why? I might have said, "Really?" I might have tried to contain the intense wanting in my voice, the desire to take all the stories he had, but he stopped me: "You know I don't like to talk about that stuff," he said. The End. How recently my mother told me, but they did know that man was White because his family used to come around, but when he died they stopped, but everybody knew, she said. Okay.

What it meant to be a Black woman and man in the segregated South, even more specifically New Orleans, and leave your home and your people, what it meant to survive and live and love and laugh fully, what it all meant if it meant anything— there was always something I couldn't quite reach in the stories my parents did or didn't tell, in the stories they thought they told, in the stories they might've told when I wasn't in the right space, when I didn't know how to listen.

I drive twelve hours the first day, so I can get through Texas, past Picacho Peak, where they reenact one of the most Western Civil War battles every year on Hohokam land, past border patrol, through lands of the Gila River, Tohono

O'odham, Pascua Yaqui, and Apache—always on Native lands, but not always thinking consciously about this.

I hate driving through Texas.

I hated driving through Texas before they murdered Sandra Bland, and before White supremacist terrorists Shawn Berry, Lawrence Russell Brewer, and John King dragged James Byrd to his death. Texas never ends. You drive and drive and you're still in Texas, and everywhere they remind you of how you're not supposed to mess with whatever lie Texas claims to be. I drive so many hours that first day to Sonora, Texas so I can be in Louisiana the next. I'm too bleary-eyed to do or think about anything, except a quick search to learn that some settler named the city of Sonora after his family servant who was from Sonora, Mexico. Later I'll learn that in September of this year, the city of Sonora will erect a marker for "La Elliot," L.W. Elliott Elementary School, a predominantly Mexican school but which also had Black students, that remained segregated until 1970, when it was finally closed after Isael Perez, Victoriano Chavez, Santos Hernandez, and Eugeno Gonzales sued on behalf of their children, sixteen years after Brown, twenty-three years after the Mendez case.

I plan to make it to Lafayette, which I do. I spend one night at the kind of B&B where everyone eats breakfast together, and where a giant painting of a mammy hangs in the kitchen. As I'm leaving the next morning, I ask the proprietor about the artist, because while the painting depicts a Black woman as mammy, the artist manages to give her some measure of humanity, meaning she's not grinning as if she's content with her servitude. The good Christian White woman educator from Texas who's staying at this same B&B, and with whom I've had pleasant if sometimes tiresome conversations rooted in deficit thinking about schooling, and who prays for me to find my keys when I lose them as I'm packing the car to leave, insists we take a picture together in front of the painting and screams, "I love mammy! I love mammy! I do!" How I want to capture the absurdity of the moment, how I'll think about this image, both the painting and the photo, and my decision to include myself in the photo, on this and future drives across the country: the lines between minstrelsy, performance, and resistance. How later I'll learn the artist is an older White woman who has other paintings of Black subjects, including another mammy painting, in which her subject also isn't smiling, but which doesn't feel as generous or humanizing to the Black woman she's supposed to be depicting, and why, when I first saw the painting, did I fool myself into almost believing the artist might've been a Black woman, and why would a White woman want to continue reconstructing Black women as mammy anyway? Not a real question.

What kind of space do I need to create to talk about the young White woman, a history major at LSU, who leads a great tour of the Laura Plantation, which is famous for being run by generations of Creole women. The guide is irreverent about the former owners and the brutal slaveowning history, which I think makes everyone on the tour, all of whom are White, uncomfortable, but makes me laugh out loud, which is what I think should happen on these plantation tours: by the end everyone should be laughing hysterically.

At one point, after explaining the Code Noir, and after talking about the way slaveholders used Black men and women as breeders, the guide and I walk to the slave cabins slightly ahead of the rest of the tour group. She asks me if I'm okay. Her question surprises me. I'd been on one other plantation tour at Nottoway, also in Louisiana, years earlier. On my tour of Nottoway, the guide didn't want to mention the word "slave" except to highlight the fact that several of the descendants of the people who had worked on the plantation (otherwise known as slaves) still worked at Nottoway. This was a selling point, evidence for the continued mythical benevolence of the Randolph family whose slaves "were probably well treated," a quote that appeared on Nottoway's website but has since been removed. And maybe this evidence of Black descendants of the enslaved employed on the current plantation was also evidence for the benevolence of all White folks everywhere who once owned or still wanted to own the slaves the guide wouldn't talk about, slaves she said she couldn't even mention until recently; and when I asked why she said, nervously, it was because they didn't have written documents verifying the identity of the slaves or they hadn't verified the documents they possessed, some ridiculous argument that made no sense. Nottoway, whose website also once said, "It is difficult to accurately assess the treatment of Randolph's slaves," but if you come for a visit, you might enjoy a lovely evening of "Murder Mystery Dinner Theater," which, "set in 1859, features Nottoway's original owners, John and Emily Randolph," and in which the "cast will even invite you to participate in solving the mystery!" Nottoway, where you still might experience the restored plantation's "days of glory." Nottoway, which still bills itself as a "Plantation & Resort."

When I go on these tours I expect erasure and invisibility. I expect, if they're using the plantation for bridal showers and weddings, to see three drunk White women, as I did at Nottoway, laugh and stagger their way to a restaurant or back to their own period decorated rooms as they walk past the "Boy's Wing," dwellings of the White sons who had their own sleeping quarters set apart from the main house for various reasons the guide may not want to mention. What kind of space do we need to create to talk about what it means to expect erasure, to prepare one's self for invisibility?

I'm surprised by the guide's question at the Laura Plantation because I didn't think anything was visible in my face that might warrant her concern. When she asks me if I'm okay, I think later that I told her I was fine, but when I look in my journal, I see that I said, "Sometimes this stuff is a lot to hear." My reason for forgetting my response is probably the same reason I head toward New Orleans instead of spending the night somewhere on River Road as I'd planned in order to visit other plantations the next day. I'm already tired. I already want to forget. Remembering is resistance. Remembering as an act of resistance takes work. Forgetting sometimes feels like salvation.

In New Orleans I spend a few days in the Tremé, where my brother has recently moved across the street from St. Augustine's, the city's oldest Black Catholic church established by free people of color. Every day I walk past *The Tomb of the Unknown Slave*, which "honors all slaves buried throughout the United States and those slaves in particular who lie beneath the ground of Tremé in unmarked, unknown graves." I walk over seashells crushed into earth and I think about ancestors, or my cousin on my father's side, who moved to the Bay Area after Katrina, and whose mother, my aunt, is living in the house my cousin was renting because a government's neglect destroyed my aunt's house in the storm. How the second day, maybe, when I'm in New Orleans, my cousin messages me to let me know her mother has suddenly been admitted to the hospital, and so my brother and I go and see her. How my Uncle Kwanza, my father's brother who will die four years later, comes to the hospital to make sure the doctors are treating my aunt well.

My other cousins are already at the hospital, cousins I haven't seen in years. They rag on my brother gently about not calling or visiting them enough. They remember me younger. They tell me I favor Ramona, one of my father's sisters who died a few months earlier, who I didn't meet that one Mardi Gras years ago because I wanted to spend time with a boy I was certain I loved. How hurt my father was, but even in his hurt anger he warned me what areas in his city were too dangerous to enter. "Stay away from the Bucket of Blood," he said, and how even in his hurt anger he let me go because he knew I was grown enough to leave. Aunt Ramona didn't say much, my sister told me later. Wore her hair in two long, black, heavy braids and seemed a little off. How the man she was married to might have hurt her, a whispered story. My aunt, who will leave the hospital after a couple of days, will later tell me my father helped pay for Ramona to go to school, sent money from California. And my cousin, the one who messaged me about my aunt being in the hospital, who will fly from the Bay and who we'll pick up at the airport, will cry when her sisters repeat to her in the house my cousin used to rent about the resemblance between me and Ramona. How my cousin will cry and say Ramona was so pretty, will cry for my aunt's gone life, for whatever whispers left in her passing.

"Doesn't she look like her?" say my cousins now. My aunt examines me from her bed. Maybe. I don't know where to look, don't know what or who they see. I want to know. Later, my cousin will text me a photo of Ramona, and another time my aunt will let me take a picture of the yellowed clipping of the announcement of Ramona's wedding at Holy Ghost soon after she graduated from Dillard, how the *bride was a vision of loveliness, white satin, teardrop pearls, veil of illusion*, but now they stare, look away and stare again. The familiar dead twinges underneath my skin. How my father will die a year and a half later but I don't know this yet.

In what space and time do I remember this?

Dear Barbara,

Enclosed is a copy of mama's death notice. Tell everyone hello.

Ramona

The morning I leave New Orleans, I hear them before I see them. I'm packing the car when rattles and bells, shaking tambourines, beating drums, whistles, chanting, and singing come from around the corner—a group of people, all Black, dressed in white, women in white headwraps and dresses, men in white pants and shirts, some shirtless. One of the men shaking a rattle is masked. I can't remember if it was a removable mask or if his face was painted. I remember his eyes looking out from something colorful. The group moves down Governor Nicholls St., the man with the mask and rattle out in front, weaving. I stand by the open trunk of my car. The masked man sidewinds his way to me, rattle in the air. A friend once told me how her father, who was from New Orleans but who died just before I met her, used to warn: "Don't let nobody ever shake anything at you in New Orleans." The masked man moves in front of me, back and forth, and shakes the rattle with feathers over my head, in front of my face, over my shoulders, over my heart, down the front of my body. I know without completely understanding that it's not the hex my friend's father warned her of, but a blessing, so I let him. I need it.

The night before, my brother and I drank wine and talked about our family, the stories we know and the stories we can't tell fully, a difficult conversation that left me exhausted. I told him stories of violence. It was his first time hearing me tell these stories. He listened. Later that night, we go to Bullet's to hear Treme Brass Band. I danced and drank and didn't think about what I don't know or what I want to know.

I close my eyes while the man shakes the rattle. I try not to cry. I'm still tired from the night before, and from being in a city where I always feel like I'm time traveling. I don't want to leave. I never want to leave New Orleans. I always leave feeling how much I don't know, and with the sense of just having missed getting to the place, to the story I need to get to.

The man finishes his blessing, and the dancers and drums and singers move to the *Tomb of the Unknown Slave* where they sing and dance their prayers of honor and remembrance. I watch for a bit from where I stand, and then go inside and tell my brother. I don't tell him about the blessing. I want to hold onto it for a bit.

My brother walks me to the car. We say goodbye. He tells me to be safe, to text him from the road so he knows I'm okay. "You gonna be okay?" he says. It's a question and a reminder. This is the brother who got me writing, who because I was bothering him when I was younger when he was trying to write while playing his records, gave me a notebook and told me to listen to the music—Stevie Wonder— and write down how it made me feel, forever linking music and writing. I turn the radio to WKOZ and cry my way out over "Do You Know What it Means" across a bridge until I hit Mississippi.

I'm at the entrance to The University of Southern Mississippi. When planning my route the night before, I looked up Hattiesburg, where in 1966 White supremacist terrorist Samuel Holloway Bowers, co-founder of the Mississippi White Knights of the Ku Klux Klan (who was born in New Orleans and died in Sunflower County, Mississippi in the Mississippi State Penitentiary) firebombed the house and grocery store where Vernon Dahmer, businessman and president of the NAACP chapter in Forrest County, created a space for Black people to pay poll taxes and register to vote, burning Dahmer so badly—almost half his body was burned, his lungs spent from smoke inhalation—that he died the next day. Dahmer's last words were a call out for his wife, Ellie, who he saved—his wife who says years later it's still "something we can't get over." Dahmer saved his wife, along with his daughters, one of whose hands were burned, and his sons, by shooting the shotguns they always had ready while his wife and children fled for safety.

White supremacist terrorist Samuel Holloway Bowers who acted with at least thirteen others—thirteen others who had to make a decision about what story they would pass down about their White family's role in the murder and terror of Black people—was finally convicted in 1998. White supremacist terrorist Samuel Holloway Bowers who was also responsible for the murders of James Earl Chaney, Andrew Goodman, and Michael H. Schwerner, all of whom disappeared from Neshoba County Jail in Philadelphia, Mississippi, and ended up dead forty-four miles somewhere else. Neshoba County Jail, the same jail where Native activist Rexdale Henry, jailed for overdue fines, will end up dead in July 2015, allegedly killed by his White cellmate Justin Schlegel, one day after they announce Sandra Bland is dead in her cell in Texas by something they're calling suicide but that looks very much like murder by cops, after a White cop arrested her for not putting out her cigarette when he asked, so for not being the slave of his wishful impoverished imagination. Neshoba County Jail, which is now housed in a different location but is still, one might could say, in a similar if not the same place it was in 1964 and 1966. In Hattiesburg, they named a street and a park for Vernon Dahmer and later they constructed a memorial. I don't go to the park because I learn about it after this trip.

The night before I left New Orleans, I read about Clyde Kennard and John Frazier, who attempted to integrate The University of Southern Mississippi, which is why I'm parked outside the entrance. I knew Medgar Evers' devastating story but not Kennard's equally heartbreaking one.

Clyde Kennard, a Korean War Veteran like my father, brother and son, attempted to enroll in The University of Southern Mississippi, back then Mississippi Southern College, to complete his degree in political science after returning home from Chicago to help his mother care for the farm after his stepfather died. He attempted to enroll three times before they jailed him, first in 1959 on trumped up speeding charges, where they said he was in possession of alcohol, and then in 1960 on false charges of theft for allegedly stealing chicken feed, a conviction that would prevent him from applying to any of the White colleges in Mississippi, but this detail is irrelevant because after they finally released him, sick with cancer, in January 1963 (mostly because of the outcry from folks like Medgar Evers), Kennard died six months later. While the official diagnosis might be intestinal cancer that generally attacked his insides, it's also true that many people and institutions with specific names, like Governor J. P. Coleman, Governor Ross Barnett, college president William D. McCain, judge T. C. Hobby, the Mississippi Supreme Court, the United States Supreme Court, and the Mississippi Sovereignty Commission, killed him.

Kennard wasn't exonerated of the false charges against him until 2006, thanks to the efforts of several dedicated people who were also involved in helping achieve the conviction of White supremacist terrorist Samuel Bowers Holloway in 1998, the same year the ACLU forced Mississippi to unseal the Sovereignty Commission, a White supremacist commission started after *Brown v. Board of Education* and abolished in 1977, but at the time of Kennard's attempts to enroll was led by Zack J. VanLandingham, a former FBI agent intent on destroying the life Kennard had and the one Kennard wanted to live.

Kennard left us a few letters he published in the *Hattiesburg American* about integration and schooling, letters in which he responds to segregationist arguments. Excerpts from his first letter published on December 6, 1958:

> Somehow I feel a great sympathy for the people who truly believe
> that the interest of both the White and Negro people would be served

best by a system of complete or partial segregation. Although I am integrationist by choice, I am a segregationist by nature, and I think most Negroes are. We prefer to be alone, but experience has taught us that if we are ever to attain the goal of first class citizenship, we must do it through a closer association with the dominant (White) group.

And later in the letter, Kennard comments on the purpose of schooling:

We believe that for men to work together best, they must be trained together in their youth. We believe that there is more to going to school than listening to the teacher and reciting lessons. In school one learns to appreciate and respect the abilities of the other.

The final letter, published on January 23, 1960, reveals the exhaustion of a man who has tried to follow unfair rules and use respectability and logic to combat a disrespectful, illogical, racist, patriarchal White supremacist system.

I have done all that is within my power to follow a reasonable course in this matter. I have wanted the State to see that our position has at least some validity. I have tried to make it clear that my love for the State of Mississippi and my hope for its peaceful prosperity is equal to any man's alive. The thought of presenting this request before a Federal Court for consideration, with all the publicity and misrepresentation which that would bring about, makes my heart heavy. Yet, what other course can I take?

Eight months after this letter, on the way back to his car after attempting to enroll for the third time, they arrest him. After they finally release him from jail, he dies on the Fourth of July, less than a month after White supremacist terrorist Byron De La Beckwith, and all of them murder Medgar Evers.

Clyde Kennard wrote a poem, "Ode to the Death Angel," in 1962, while he was still imprisoned, or three days before his death according to other sources, the same year James Meredith fought to be admitted to The University of Mississippi:

Oh here you come again
Old chilly death of Ol'
To plot out life
And test immortal soul

I saw you fall against the raging sea
I cheated you then and now you'll not catch me
I know your face
It's known in every race
Your speed is fast
And along the way
Your shadow you cast

High in the sky
You thought you had me then
I landed safely
But here you are again

I see you paused upon that forward pew
When you think I'm asleep
I'm watching you
Why must you hound me so everywhere I go?
It's true my eyes are dim
My hands are growing cold
Well take me on then, that
I might at last become my soul

Sometimes when I read Kennard's poem I replace "death" with "Whiteness" or White Supremacy."

After Clyde Kennard, John Frazier also attempted to enroll at the university in March of 1964, but they turned him away. One part of Frazier's story that gets me is when he first attempted to enroll, the college newspaper took a photo of him and did a brief write-up. That same day, USM president, McCain, ordered people to confiscate all of the papers, and so they went into classrooms and took them from students, did whatever they needed to do, and then burned them. They re-ran the paper without Frazier's story. Just like that, erased, but student staff at the *Student Printz* saved copies of both papers, the truth and the lie.

Raylawni Branch and Gwendolyn Elaine Armstrong Chamberlain were the first Black people to enroll at The University of Southern Mississippi. In 1965. Only two years after Clyde Kennard's death.

It takes about three hours and some change to drive from Hattiesburg, Mississippi to Birmingham, Alabama. You might be tempted to take the road to Montgomery, which will have you pass through Selma, and then maybe take the hour-and-twenty drive up to Birmingham. Years down the road, you might regret not taking this route because when will you pass this way again? When will you ever cross the Edmund Pettus Bridge, where Obama will give a speech on the fiftieth anniversary of Bloody Sunday, a speech that acknowledges the changes we've made as a country as well as the injustice documented in the Ferguson Report and the work we still need to do, and at the same time enumerates who we are as a country while violently erasing our settler colonial past and present, as in "We're the ranch hands and cowboys who opened up the West"? A speech where he says, "We respect the past, but we don't pine for the past."

But it might be later in the day than you planned. The Civil Rights Institute stops selling tickets at 4:30. You have to get on. Take the 59N toward Laurel for about eighty-three miles and continue on I-20E for about 150 miles more. You won't remember much of this drive, lots of green on the side of the highways maybe, but you might be confusing this with the green and swamp you felt leaving New Orleans. When you drive this long the radio turns into nothing so you turn it off, or you listen to one song like Brand Nubian's "U for Me" over and over until you almost get the words down to that one verse about Harriet Tubman. You'll pass signs for cities like Meridian, which will make you think of Alice Walker and the novel you should probably re-read. Take exit 125A onto 17th Street toward downtown and you'll hit Kelly Ingram Park.

When you were younger, Birmingham was a huge and terrifying place you never wanted to see if you thought about it at all, which was probably only once a year during Black History Month, but then a family from Birmingham moved in next door with a son your age, who you first thought was so country with his flooded green corduroys he had to wear until his real clothes arrived and the way he said "'Bama," and then his dimples did you in, but even that didn't completely erase the messed up things you thought about the South. If anything, your neighbor's family leaving Birmingham for California was further evidence the South was a place you left if you could, and when this family returned to Alabama several years later it provided more proof, along with one of your early memories of the French Quarter and the joy you often heard in your parents' stories about New Orleans, that along with their silences, whatever fear and horror existed in the South there was also something beautiful and Black.

You watched the footage every year on TV: Bull Connor, water hoses, dogs, Black children flying from the force of the water hoses held by grown White men who made it hard to believe they might have been somebody's children once or had chil-

dren of their own. But here you are in Birmingham and everything seems so small, the dollhouse version of the Civil Rights Movement. Kelly Ingram Park, where so many of the protests took place, is little more than an acre. It makes you think, not for the first time, about the intimacy of violence, the way people had to walk around a small city knowing their neighbor was their murderer, the way murderers walked free for years looking past the eyes of the surviving families of the people they killed. You think about your parents' desire to leave their community in New Orleans where people knew you, for better or for worse.

The 16th Street Baptist Church where White supremacist terrorists Bobby Frank Cherry, Thomas Blanton, Robert Chambliss, and Herman Frank Cash planted a bomb, which resulted in the murders of Addie Mae Collins, Cynthia Wesley, Carole Robertson, and Denise McNair, sits on a corner across the street from the park.

All that horror happened here?

How Cherry, Blanton, and Chambliss weren't convicted until 1977, 2001, and 2002, and Cash never was—he died in 1994. How Sarah Collins Rudolph, who was just twelve years old and who was with her older sister Addie Mae, and who lost her right eye and had "twenty-six pieces of glass" removed from her face, with glass also lodged in "her chest and stomach," remembers the past Obama says we respect but don't pine for. "I still shake," she says. "I still jump when I hear loud sounds." Sarah Collins Rudolph says, "Every day I think about it, just looking in the mirror and seeing the scars on my face. I'm reminded of it every day." The city of Birmingham has yet to compensate Sarah Collins Rudolph for the eye they took, and for her other remaining scars.

The church is locked so you can't go inside. You're hungry. A man sitting at the top of the church steps tells you where you can get some good fried chicken.

Before you eat, you go to the Civil Rights Institute, which sits across from the park and the church. There are lots of tour buses with church groups. Before you enter the exhibits an older male ticket taker asked you, "You here by yourself?" You get this a lot on this trip and others you'll take. A Black woman traveling alone is and has always been both invisible and highly suspect. When you get the question from other Black folk, some of that is present, but depending on who's saying it it's more about concern and care, more about, "Who and where are your people?"

Moving through the Institute is a blur: photographs, videos, audio, objects underneath glass cases—a violent history contained. It reminds you of Manzanar where you went years earlier, a detour on a return trip from Nevada to California, which was around the same period of time when you were feeling compelled to visit so-called Missions throughout California whose primary mission was, of course, the stealing of land, further attempts at genocide, and terror of Indigenous peoples. All of this years before you knew you were writing anything about remembering and forgetting. When you think about that visit to Manzanar, what you remember is an outdoor graveyard with a monument whose Japanese inscription translates to "Soul Consoling Tower"; you see the foothills of the Sierras off in the distance, and the arid land where the U.S. forced the Owens Valley Paiute to walk hundreds of miles to Fort Tejon, just forty-two years before L.A. began buying water rights in the Owens Valley, so the city in which you were born and raised could continue existing, just seventy-nine years before the U.S. Army leased the abandoned, now bone-dry land from L.A. and forced Japanese Americans into the concentration camp of Manzanar; you think about euphemisms like *internment, evacuation, relocation, assembly and reception center*, and you remember walking through the exhibit at Manzanar and seeing a pair of baby shoes underneath a glass case similar to the glass cases you're walking past now, but there were so many items, you could be inventing those baby shoes.

You keep walking through the Institute, each exhibit blurring into the next.

When you return to the Civil Rights Institute in summer 2016 on a drive from Michigan to Louisiana to New Mexico, you realize as you walk through the Institute again that you didn't remember, or you blocked out, one of the last displays in the exhibit—a caseholding items that Denise McNair had with her when she was murdered: the purse, small bracelet, dress shoes stuffed with tissue paper, and the piece of brick that was lodged in her skull. And visiting 16th Street Baptist Church on the one-year anniversary of the Charleston Church Massacre right before walking through the institute, and then seeing these small items of a little girl who should still be alive breaks you, and you're also thinking about the victims of the mass murder at Pulse just a few days earlier, and the survivors; and you're also thinking how when you and your husband returned to the U.S. from Jamaica a few weeks earlier, and were heading up the escalator out of Customs, one of the first things you see is a White man on the next escalator wearing a backpack with a confederate flag patch stitched on the back, and the Black man a few steps ahead of you on the escalator takes out his camera and looks behind him to check to see if anyone else sees what he's seeing and sees you and your husband watching him watching Mr. Confederacy, and you all shake your heads and laugh in disbelief at your welcome home to the U.S., and he takes his picture of White Power and you take yours; and when you walk through the Civil Rights Institute you're following a group of Black kids, around five or six years old, getting a tour, and when the tour guide asks them to shout what country they live in, they all shout, Alabama!! And the day before, at the 16th Street church you think again how the legacies of violence in this country are long and don't always wear the visible badge of the confederacy, and there have never been any true sanctuaries, but that still won't stop you/us from living and loving and making space and centering ourselves when and where we can, and calling a state a country because we know.

But on this 2010 walk through the Institute, you won't remember much of anything. You need coffee.

You walk through the historic district past the old vaudeville Lyric theatre on 3rd Avenue, which, of course, used to be segregated, and then back up the same street toward your car. You've almost given up on finding coffee when a kind man on a bicycle whose name you can't remember tells you you should go to Z's Take-Out Restaurant on 17th Street N. He takes you to Z's, which you're not far from, and when you open the door of the restaurant the man on the bike leans in and yells to the man at the counter that he's got this one. "I got this," he says. You say it's okay, there's no need, but he tells the man to put it on him. Still planning to pay, you thank him and he rides away. Then there is this:

The best bean pie you've ever eaten. The kind of bean pie that when you get in your car you call your husband and yell about. The kind of bean pie you think about sending a thank-you postcard to the restaurant for—not only for the pie, which is cold and just sweet enough, but also for the fresh pot of coffee the older gentleman makes for you along with the extra piece of bean pie he gives all on the house, even though you try to pay, but he shakes his head and says the man on the bike has got it, all of which helps you get through most of Tennessee. The kind of bean pie that

doesn't make you forget poverty or class and skin privilege and everything that's made and making it possible for you to be in this restaurant on 17th street in Birmingham, and it doesn't make you forget four little Black girls and counting, all of whom should still be living, but the kind of bean pie that reminds you who your people are, that lets you remember Black love and kindness that sustains.

You should stop in Chattanooga, which looks pretty from the road, but you're tired. You keep driving and stay in a roadside hotel near Knoxville that costs too much. You flip through the hotel guidebook, a little whacked out from driving eight hours, and you learn about the Ramsey House Plantation, which was built "by one of the first families to settle the Knoxville area." (Drink every time a historical site uses the word "settle.")

The website says school tours cover "Architecture, Butter Churning, Corn Husk Dolls, Candle Dipping, Slavery, Surveying, and Toys and Games." Despite the quotidian nature of the list, you're glad at least slavery is included. Somehow you

miss noting the hours of operation. The next morning you drive out to the planta-
tion, but it's closed and so you kick the fence and hate the lush green leading up to
the main house because plantations are always on grotesque, stunning land. *Boys
hanging from the most beautiful sycamores in the world.* All that horror happened here.
You get back in the car and drive.

   This is all to say by the time I reach Virginia I'm tired and through—with history,
with the coded language we use to describe atrocities that have made this country
and particular individuals and their descendants wealthy. I'm tired of my own privi-
lege and arrogance in believing the language I might use to tell stories about any of it,
language born out of this history, will be any better, any more succinct or expansive.

Blacksburg, Virginia

   Smithfield Plantation. The Fourth of July. I've just missed a flag ceremony in the
parking area at the entrance to the plantation. White men are dressed in American
Revolutionary uniforms, and White women wear white bonnets and ruffled shirts
and skirts. *What the fuck? Where the fuck am I?* There might be the lingering scent
of gunsmoke in the air from muskets being fired, but maybe I'm making that up. I
don't remember for sure. Smithfield, which I later learn sits on lands of the Tutelo/
Monacan Nations. I pay for my ticket to the tour in the museum gift shop, and then
stand on the back porch of the main house, which overlooks a garden. Beyond the

garden is a field, and beyond the field, a highway. When the tour begins, I'll learn they think the field is where slave cabins stood, but on another tour I'll take of this same plantation in a different year I'll learn they believe slave cabins sat in the field at the front of the house, which I walked past on my way to the gift shop. This makes more sense. I can imagine William Preston and his slaveowning heirs, standing on the front steps of his grand house and surveying everything they believed they owned: trees, earth, slaves.

Other people, all White, also wait on the porch for the tour to begin. A young White man leads the tour. He's supposed to be in costume. He's wearing a black vest over what might be a blousy white shirt, but all I really remember is his black vest, which I think resembles a regular vest. His black vest and his bored expression are the pieces that stay with me, and the way he recites stories about the slaveowning Preston family as if someone's forcing him to read from a seventh grade textbook.

We move through the different rooms: the foyer, the owner's bedroom, and the dining room. The guide doesn't mention slavery on the tour until he shows the up-stairs rooms where the slaveowner's children may have slept. Slave girls and women may have slept on a pallet in the small hallway in order to care for the children, he says. I think about the ways this put enslaved girls and women in danger. I think about who had access to them. I think about power and silence.

In what may have been the children's bedroom, the guide points to a handmade doll crib. He says a male slave built this crib as a gift for the family. "Would a slave create something for his master's children if he didn't like his master?" he says. I'm stunned by the stupidity of the question, and by stupidity I mean the lack of critical understanding of power, race, racism, White supremacy, and slavery. I think about some White people and institutions I've worked for. I think about tasks I've completed with or without a smile, gifts I might've given, all the while engaging in the liberatory practice of imagining killing or maiming, self-defense, self-love, and long-term freedom. No one in the tour group resists this guide's interpretation of the slave's supposed happiness, nor do I. It hasn't been that long since I kicked the fence of the closed plantation in Tennessee. It's hard to believe only yesterday I was at a museum that documents the history of the Civil Rights Movement.

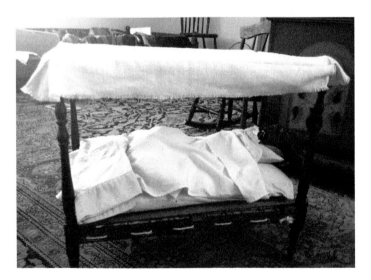

We reach the kitchen room in the basement. The kitchen room is filled with kitchen artifacts. Herbs hang over the large fireplace, within which sit cast iron cookware. In front of the fireplace is a wooden table with various tools used for cooking arranged on top of the table. Then, I see her. I don't remember exactly when I notice her, but when I think about first walking into this room she's what I see to the right of the fireplace. A mannequin, a slave mannequin.

Not a full mannequin, not a full slave. Just a torso. Armless. She's dressed in what's supposed to be slave garb: white kerchief on her head, a long white apron over a mustard top, and underneath the mustard top a white frock. Since she has no arms, the sleeves of her dress hang hollow at her sides. Her face is masked beneath a dark brown stocking. It could be easy to ignore her because along with all the other artifacts she's just another thing. It could be easy if you weren't thinking about the person or people she's supposed to represent.

A broom is attached to the wall behind the slave mannequin. She stands next to a round wooden slab. On top of the slab rests a metal rod, a tool enslaved people used to beat dough. The disaffected guide displays the rod and invites people to hold it to feel its weight. Adults and children brandish the metal rod. The tour group marvels at the strength the person must have possessed to beat dough with a rod so heavy. I think, she has no arms. *She has no arms.* Later I'll think, there's a mannequin of a Black woman who's supposed to represent an enslaved person on a tour where slavery and enslaved people are barely mentioned, and only in the service of maintaining the myth of the benevolent slaveholder. Her stockinged face and missing arms say so much about the silence about slavery on the tour and in our national conversation, and the way racism and White Supremacy relegate Black women to positions where people display us in the service of institutions but demand our silence and our bodies. I don't take a picture of her.

The tour ends. I'm done with plantations on this trip. Done.

I eventually land in Auburn, New York. I drive by the Auburn Correctional Facility, which sits on Cayuga land, and is the site of the first execution by electric chair. I stay in a hotel that has seen better days. I eat good Italian food. I go to the Harriet Tubman Home for the Aged, a resting place she created for the elderly and those in need, and where she died in 1913. The bottom floor of the Home for the Aged is open to tour. During the time I visit, the home in which Harriet actually lived is closed, in disrepair. The barn was restored because it was in danger of falling down. The guide tells me Harriet's house will probably be restored next. At the time, the site is a National Historic Landmark. In seven years it will become a National Park. The caretaker and the guides are doing so much to care for the property with very little outside assistance. I think, again, about well-preserved, well-funded plantations, and what it says about what this country wants to remember, what it romanticizes, and what it wishes would disappear.

I go to Fort Hill Cemetery and sit for a while at Harriet Tubman's grave, two U.S. flags stuck in the ground on either side of the headstone. I add a small rock to her headstone in between two other rocks, offerings from others. I say thank you, I ask for some things, I make some promises. I write a little bit about how only two days earlier I was at a plantation. *Where in this country is it not a graveyard?* It's not a real question.

I head to the Whitest state in the Union, where I'll visit a house that people say may have been a spot on the Underground Railroad.

I'm still not sure what I'm doing.

December 2011

My father passes. I find out about his passing when I return from a weekend near Lake Michigan with a friend who's visiting us. I've been in Michigan for about four and a half months. I've begun a job as an Assistant Professor of Creative Writing in an English Department whose chairs have only been White men. The amount of what many people call micro-aggressions, but which I just call aggressions because there's nothing micro about them, is stifling. Toward the end of the semester, in another department, someone finds a Black doll hanging by a noose. I'm ready for the holiday break. We take our friend to the airport, and when we return, I open my inbox to a string of emails about when my brothers and sisters are returning home. Emails about funeral arrangements. Emails about the obituary. My father is dead. He's been ill for a while and now he's dead. There's a message on my phone from one of my sisters. I talk to my mother. I buy a plane ticket to California. I begin the long process of grieving. My grieving becomes part of the work of writing. My writing becomes part of the work of grieving. I'm not sure work is the best description. Whatever it is—this work, this writing, this remembering—it isn't any different than what I've already been doing, just more pronounced.

Before news of my father's death I'd purchased tickets to New Orleans. I still go after the funeral, leaving my immediate family, and spend Christmas with my husband, cousins, and aunt—my father's sister—the one who was in the hospital in 2010. In the airport, on the way to L.A., and then to New Orleans, twice I almost walk into the men's bathroom. The first time I catch myself, but the second time I get far enough inside where a man coming out of the doorway I'm about to enter shakes his head at me, looking concerned. "No," he says. "No." I'm dazed, not sure what I'm thinking about.

While in New Orleans, my husband and I get off the streetcar and are waiting on neutral ground for cars to pass in order to cross the street to walk to my aunt's house. I move to step in the street, but my husband yanks me back. "Hey," he says. "What are you doing?" Cars fly by. "I wasn't looking," I say. Maybe I laugh so he won't worry. Maybe I think, wake up, wake up. I don't know what I'm thinking. Dazed, a haze that will cover me for at least a year. We spend time with my aunt and my Uncle Kwanza, the one who will die in four years. 2011 passes somehow. I teach. I go places. I do things. I couldn't care less about the novel I've been working on.

Blacksburg, Virginia, 2012

I attend an event at Virginia Tech celebrating Toni Morrison. The event is titled "Sheer Good Fortune," echoing the epigraph in Morrison's *Sula*: "It is sheer good fortune to miss somebody long before they leave you." The book is dedicated to her sons, one of whom, Slade, passed in 2010. The goal of the event, organized by Nikki Giovanni, Joanne Gabbin, and Maya Angelou, is to honor Morrison's life and work while she's still living.

I fly into Roanoke and drive to Blacksburg through the vivid red, orange, and yellow leaves of the changing season. Around this time next year, a doctor will tell me there is something that appears cancerous in my thyroid. By the time I get this news, I will have already read about Black women having more advanced cases of thyroid cancer. I will have already read about this autoimmune thing that's creating antibodies to attack my body, which has been feeling off, but I'm not sure if it's just grief. In a year, I'll begin preparing for a surgery scheduled three days after the one-year anniversary of my father's passing, but again, I don't know any of this yet.

I stay at a hotel downtown. The next morning I go on another tour of Smithfield Plantation. This time I'm the only one on the tour. The tour guide is an older White woman wearing a Betsy Ross bonnet. She leads me through the same rooms as in the last tour. She tells the same stories. She barely mentions slavery. This time I take pictures of all the rooms. I take pictures of the handmade doll crib, the plastic fruit, the stairs leading up to where the children may have slept, and where enslaved girls may have slept outside the children's bedroom.

Later, I write field notes. My husband, who is an ethnographer, tells me that generally field notes are done within twenty-four hours of an interview or a site visit, otherwise you can't really trust your memory, and he reminds me of what I know about writing, that in the process of recalling what happened I'll remember more details. I'm still not completely sure what it is I'm doing at this plantation, but I want to remember. I do know I'm here to see the slave mannequin again.

From my notes:

Near the end of the tour she offers the info that the slaveowner authored a bill to secede from union. She tries to buffer this by saying he understood that if all the slaves were freed at once then the economy would collapse. He believed in state's rights, she says.

"But there's the issue of human rights," I say.

"I know. I know," she says. "Well, there's that."

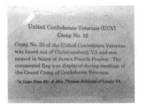 

The slave mannequin still stands in the kitchen. I take pictures. The guide offers me the metal rod used to beat bread. I hold it, feel its weight. I take more pictures. I want to remember.

Later that evening I listen to Toni Morrison say, "Once you get the White man out of your book, the whole world opens up; you can begin to think about real things, not just respond to stereotypes."

After the ceremony, I walk past the memorial to the thirty-two students murdered in the 2007 shooting, the raised mini coffins lit with soft light.

Blacksburg, Virginia, February 2013

I'm awarded a writing residency at Atlantic Center for the Arts (ACA) in Florida. I'm going to be in a prose and poetry workshop facilitated by a White poet whose work around poetry of witness I learned about when I was in graduate school many years earlier, and whose work has taught me to consider what a poem (and writer) can do and be, work that is part of a long history and a long line of poets. I'm thinking particularly of Black women writers like June Jordan, whose classes I took when I was an undergraduate, and Jordan's poems about police violence, and her work on Black language, and her essays and her fiction. Jordan, who died of cancer in 2002, who believed that poetry was and always has been for the people, that anyone can write poetry, and that poetry needs to tell the truth. Poetry of witness is part of this history. Black women have always been witnesses to the terror in this anti-Black, settler colonial nation, and our witnessing is an active state. *Can I get a witness?* The poet leading the ACA workshop is someone whose work has also encouraged me to question what it means to be a witness, the power and privilege involved when one is witnessing the terror of a group that one may not be a part of. Who gets to tell the story? Who do we compensate for this labor? How might I be implicated in reproducing terror?

I don't have to teach this semester. I'm relieved.

I drive to Florida from East Lansing. On my way, I stop at Smithfield again. I go on another tour. This time it's different. I feel it before I leave the car.

From my notes:

In the parking lot, I'm in the car. It's light snow outside. I feel dread, maybe not so much dread as just tired. I'm tired of coming to this place. Smithfield. I know what I'm going to hear on the tour and I don't want to hear it. I know that I'll have to say something this time. I know it already, that something will be said that is wrong, inaccurate, hurtful, and I will not be able to not say something. This makes me tired . . .

The door to the gift shop is locked. I'm annoyed. The least the plantation can do is be open when it says it's going to be open. I call the number. The woman who answers the phone tells me to meet her at the front of the house, at the front door. I walk up the front steps. The door is open. The tour guide is a young White woman. It feels strange to enter the plantation through the front door.

Notes:

I can't remember what questions I asked her when we were standing in the foyer, if I asked her more questions about the slaves. I feel as if I did because I think our conversation was continuing as we moved into the next room. When we moved into the next room, which is the Prestons' bedroom as well as the guest bedroom, the guide mentioned something about the registry of slave names that was recently discovered, maybe in the last five years or so. So not that recent but recent enough. The registry had been stuck inside some other book and it had been discovered, I think, by a professor at VTech. The registry includes the names of slaves of every county in Virginia (I think). The guide says they now have the names of the slaves that the Prestons owned. She then proceeds to tell this amazing story about two of the men, two brothers: Thomas Fraction and Othello Fraction. The guide mentioned something about their last names, the possibility that it came from the fact that they were considered a fraction of a human being, but she said they don't know for sure.

Othello and Thomas Fraction are two whole men, brothers and slaves.
They join the Union army, the 40th U.S. Colored Troops.

This tour ends up being filled with stories about the enslaved people who lived on the plantation. The guide loves history and tells the narratives of those the Preston family enslaved with the energy and care of someone who understands the importance of small stories in revealing a larger history. The stories are incredible and difficult. When the guide sees my responses to some of the stories, responses that sometimes include an audible "Oh my God," or "Jesus," or a closing of my eyes and breathing in and out and shaking my head, she pauses, seemingly startled, as if she's realizing even more, or maybe for the first time, the legacy and impact of these stories that are about real people. I'm taking notes. I want to remember. We go to the kitchen room.

Notes:

But this time when we stand in front of the fireplace the guide says, "This is Sookie."

The mannequin has a name!! I repeat the name. "Sookie?" I say. I ask her to spell it.

"S-U-C-K-Y," she says.

That it actually spells "sucky" is just too much. As in, "It is sucky that she's a faceless mannequin," or "Smithfield Plantation is sucky."

Sucky was the head cook. She's on a registry list, which is hung sometimes on one of the walls but is upstairs.

Next to Sucky is a wooden block and on top of the block is the metal rod used to beat dough. The guide gives it to me to hold. The guide says when she gives tours to groups of kids one of the children will inevitably ask about Sucky, "Is that what they used to beat her?"

I think the guide sees this story as cute, as in, kids just wouldn't know any better. But I think, they know enough to know enslaved people were beat. I don't think it's cute. I think it's awful. "Oh God," I say. Then the guide proceeds to say that there is no evidence of the Prestons beating their slaves.

"That doesn't mean it didn't happen," I say.

"Oh, of course," she says.

But she then talks about nearby plantations where they do have evidence of horrible beatings that took place. "Have you heard of the hanging tree?" she says.

"No," I say. "That doesn't sound good."

She tells where this tree was, which plantation [In my notes is a question mark noting I don't remember the name of the plantation.]. "Well no one was ever hung from it, but they used it as a threat."

This sounds suspect to me. Then she says something about the Prestons being kind to their slaves.

I finally ask. "Can I ask you something?" I say.

She looks worried. "Sure?" she says, nodding.

"Has anyone ever questioned that there's a mannequin of a faceless Black woman in here?

The guide's eyes open wider. She's been giving me this look throughout the tour when I ask questions or when I contradict one of her interpretations. "No," she says.

I tell her my own reaction when I first came on the tour, how it bothered me, but how the second time I was glad she [Sucky] was there because at least there was some representation of the slaves. Since very little mention was made of the enslaved people on the tours, I re-saw her presence as filling in that gap. But I said I was torn about it still.

"I've never thought about it," she says. "But now that you say it, I think, 'oh, she's faceless.'"

I tell her again I'm torn about the mannequin's presence. She tells me to think more about it and to let her know what I think should be said or done. I tell her, "I guess if she was presented in the context of 'we don't know a lot of the stories about the slaves and so we have her here to represent the stories we don't know, then that would be better. Better than just saying 'This is Sucky.'"

The guide says she is responsible for what gets said on the tours and she can tell the story of my asking the question and talk about that in the tours. "That would be good," I say.

I can't remember what else we talk about, but she tells me she has the registry that has Sucky's name upstairs and she can show it to me if I'd like. I haven't seen these rooms because they're used as offices, and so I say yes, but also because I want to see Sucky's name.

This is the kitchen: baskets, dried herbs, cast iron pots, pans, and Sucky. Sucky is a mannequin, her stockinged face faceless.

We go upstairs and she shows me the large poster that has Sucky's name along with other names. One of the names listed is my own full [first] name: Rachel. . . .

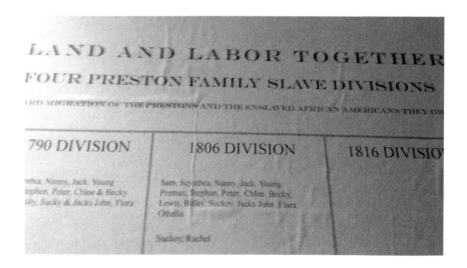

The guide and I talk more. I let her know this was one of the best plantation tours I've been on, that she knows so much, and she tells the stories so well. She tells me to email her anytime with any thoughts or suggestions.

When the tour ends, she walks me out, again through the front door. This is when I learn the new info about the slave cabins not being beyond the back porch as they had once thought. The guide points out a tree in the field, says it's over five hundred years old.

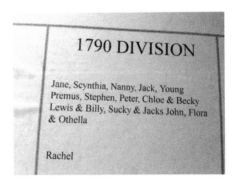

1790 DIVISION

Jane, Scynthia, Nanny, Jack, Young
Premus, Stephen, Peter, Chloe & Becky
Lewis & Billy, Sucky & Jacks John, Flora
& Othella

Rachel

Notes:

I thank [the guide] and she shuts the door, and I walk down the path to the tree. It's massive. I walk around the tree. The trunk is so large that when I stand behind it I don't think I can be seen from the house. Snow starts falling soft at first and then thicker. It's cold. I take pictures of the

tree and the field, trying to capture all of this, the height and thickness, and weight of the tree, the ghostly winter field, the highway off in the distance, the feeling of the plantation house looming over it all, but the pictures don't do it justice. Nothing can. Sucky.

New Smyrna Beach, Florida, February 2013

In Florida at ACA, I plan to write an essay about the travel through the South, and the visits to the plantation. I've brought a very rough draft of what will become "On Forgetting" with me, but in the course of the workshop my writing begins to resemble something closer to poetry.

One of the first exercises is to write a poem from a list of forty words the poet gives us. The goal of the exercise, or one of the goals, is to consider the ways we might use language to create unexpected images and meanings. I write a simple poem about stages of grief. The first poem I've written in years. It's a small opening, all I need to start putting some of this grief on the page.

At some point I realize I'm close to Sanford, where George Zimmerman shot and murdered Trayvon Martin. The residency coincides with the one-year anniversary of Trayvon Martin's death, February 26.

New Smyrna Beach is 91% White.

The artists in residence are predominantly White. My workshop is supportive and challenging in most the ways I need it to be, and still I am the only Black person, and the only person of color, which always matters. I drink a lot and dance and eat a lot of oysters. I remember what the guide at Smithfield told me about the hanging tree on the neighboring plantation. Instead of writing the essay I thought I was going to write, I stumble across advertisements for runaway enslaved people from Virginia. I've read advertisements like these before, but what strikes me this time is slaveholders' disbelief that the people they're trying very hard to regard as property might have agency and have exerted their power by running away, and alongside this disbelief are physical descriptions that include mutilation of the enslaved person's body, which provides some evidence for one possible reason for escape, and alongside these descriptions and underneath this disbelief is a seeping fear on the part of slaveowners. What I also hear in these advertisements is the genius of Black resistance—the plotting, the stealing of clothes, the fighting back.

I use colored pencils to code each advertisement: pink for whether the enslaved was a Negro man or boy or mulatto wench; white for the name the slaveholder gave them; light green for whatever scars have happened upon their bodies—burned ears, scars over eyebrows, whippings on backs; light blue for what the enslaved person took when he/she ran, and so on. I write other things that might be poems, still not sure what I'm doing.

When I workshop the incomplete essay, and when I talk with the workshop group about the places I've been—New Orleans, the plantation, the mannequin—the poet asks me if I know why I'm doing this. *Why are you doing this?* she says. To go to a plantation one time, okay, but to keep going, there have to be other reasons. Later that evening, she'll tell me I have to admit returning to this plantation is a little weird. In the same conversation, she'll tell about her visits to Monticello, rapist White supremacist Thomas Jefferson's tortuous playground (which I'll end up going to at some point), but as she's talking about her visits to Jefferson's plantation, it becomes clear she's been there more than once. "Wait," I'll say. I'll ask her how many times, and she'll say over ten or eleven. She's not exactly sure. We'll laugh.

In workshop, when she asks why I'm doing this, I feel the sudden claustrophobia that comes over me in certain situations, a specific closing-in feeling I know is very much connected to the stories of violence I talked about with my brother in New Orleans. I know what she's asking, but I say the easy answer first, something like, you mean other than that we need to name these historical atrocities because the same violence is enacted in the present? Yes, she says, why else?

To really answer her question, I'd have to acknowledge stories of violence in my family. I'd have to talk about the conversation I had with my brother in New Orleans on the drive I took in 2010, how he said he had no idea about these stories. "But how could you not know?" I said, even as I knew how easy it is for any of us to not want to know about violence, historical or personal, how easy it is to look away or call it something else, how for a long time I didn't think of my stories as violence; and, I'd also feel a compulsion to specify to my workshop that my father is not responsible for these particular stories I'm thinking about, because whatever his own personal trauma, my father made sure to protect and love me in the best way he could, but I'd also have to explain that, while he's not directly responsible, the legacy of his own trauma and his silence about his trauma preceded and followed him in such a way where he does bear some responsibility; and I'd also have to acknowledge how my urge to protect my father even in death is rooted in a relentless patriarchy that protects cishet Black men and murders cis and trans Black women in more ways than I have breath to name; and that my journeys to this plantation, and to lynching sites, and gravesites, and unmarked places where Black brilliance once lived is connected to many things, including but not limited to legacies of sexual violence, personal and historical. I'd also have to say some of these stories are not mine to tell.

As much as I love this poet and this poet's work, this workshop, where I am the only Black person, is not the space for this conversation. In this workshop, where we haven't interrogated racism or White Supremacy or anti-Blackness and all of its intersections, her question feels violent. So in response, I say something simple but still true about silences in stories, something about my parents, something about New Orleans. I don't really remember what I say. The room is quiet and a little tense. Her response: And if you name those silences, then things might unravel in your family, is that right? She's not looking at me when she says this, and so I know she understands. Yes, I say. I don't remember how we move to whatever comes next. We change the topic because that's what we often do in these moments, but I'm still stuck in the question. *Why are you doing this?*

The essay I thought I was going to write feels like a lie because it is. While it might be possible to write about historical violence without telling stories of personal violence, for this essay it's a giant hole I'm writing around and it shows. I won't touch the essay for a few years. I'll write more poems. When I return to the essay I'll think about the poet's question, a question I, of course, considered more than once prior to ending up in a workshop in a city only forty minutes from where Zimmerman murdered Trayvon Martin. And I'll think about the ways the poet's question in that particular moment, similar to the poem I wrote about stages of grief, created a small opening, an opening that allows me to at least acknowledge in a small public way that these stories of violence exist; and, eventually, this will lead me to space where I'll accept that any attempt to tell stories of this cis-hetero, patriarchal, White supremacist, settler colonial nation state can't happen without also telling the stories of sexual violence that were part and parcel in the forming and continued development of this nation, stories that Black women, Indigenous women, and other women of color have been telling for as long as we've been breathing, stories that reverberate across generations.

Question from Anonymous Reader: *Is she searching American history for the source of the family (sexual) violence that she has endured (which is only obliquely referenced and never mentioned again)? Is she trying to unearth the silent history of racist terrorism that predated her, and her father, but that profoundly affected them both? Is she vowing to dig up the untold stories of interpersonal and community violence wrought by white supremacists against countless, nameless African Americans? If so, how are these linked...*

Yes. Yes. Yes.

Answer to Anonymous Reader: *The silent history of racist terrorism that predated her, and her father, but that profoundly affected them both is part of the American history that is part of the source of the family (sexual) violence that she has endured, which can only be obliquely referenced and never mentioned again even as she makes a vow to continue to dig up the untold stories of interpersonal and community violence wrought by white supremacists against countless, so-called nameless African Americans.*

There is going to be a final performance at the residency where the public is invited. I want to read something that allows me to speak Trayvon Martin's name in this White city and White space. Trayvon's murder, my visits to Smithfield and to other sites of terror, all the stories about the enslaved the guide has shared, and my father's death are linked, but I'm not sure how this linking will appear and sound on the page.

Because your year-old death hangs fresh with other deaths I know, old and new: my father, Oscar Grant, Troy Davis.

A couple of days before the reading, I still haven't written anything for the final performance. I'm stressed. There are too many stories in my head, too many voices. I don't want to appropriate Trayvon Martin's death, if that's even the right word. There's always so much at stake and I don't wanna fuck it up. I lie in bed. I close my eyes and repeat Trayvon's name. I repeat the word "plantation." I'm hoping the link between the two will somehow emerge through naming, through breath: plantation Trayvon plantation Trayvon plantation plantation Trayvon Trayvon ...

Meet me on the plantation steps.

How after I read the poem dedicated to Trayvon Martin, a White woman who lives in New Smyrna Beach will ask me, Is New Smyrna Beach really 91% White? Another White woman will ask me, Did you know Trayvon? It sounded like you knew him. Someone will say thank you. Someone will say that was so moving. Someone will say I wanted to cry. A woman of color will say, I think I can write about my brother's death now. I realized I could do this after you read. A White man affiliated with the residency will tell me: It's been hard on the entire community, and I'll think no no, it's not the same. If you're still breathing, if your children are alive and living without fear, it's not the same. No.

⚓

Later this same year I drive to Georgia for another residency and on the way, in Kentucky, I get a call from the nurse saying yes, they were wrong before, and there is something in my body attacking itself, but they still will not have identified the cancer, and I won't need science to tell me the war my body is waging against itself is connected to historical and personal stories of violence.

How while I'm in Georgia working on a novel, I'll plan a trip to Beaufort, South Carolina, after I learn Sista Docta Alexis Pauline Gumbs, who I don't know yet, is planning a Black feminist retreat for queer Black feminists and their allies in honor of the 150th anniversary of Harriett Tubman's freeing of hundreds of enslaved people at the Combahee River.

How we'll stay at the Penn Center where the newly freed were educated, where the house Martin Luther King Jr. stayed in while working on his "I Have a Dream" speech is closed, but I stand on the porch and peek in the dusty windows and wonder, how the house they built for King closer to the water is down a trail past an old cemetery, how he never got to stay there.

How when I tell Alexis about Black Space, a digital space I made in fall 2012, Alexis will tell me about Erna Brodber, a Black Jamaican woman, who has been thinking and writing and doing Black Space as a private space and place where Black Jamaicans "can talk to each other and find out for ourselves about each other" away from Whiteness, how she has been doing this for years.

How it will remind me of being in Georgia on the way to South Carolina, passing faded, rusty signs marking Alice Walker land, and pristine monuments to Flannery O'Connor, and the old slave cabin where Uncle Remus is preserved, and how when I walk into the museum, which is actually made up of three slave cabins, I'm greeted with audio recordings of Joel Chandler Harris stories filled with N-Words, and one of the White women working behind the counter will kindly put me on the phone with Ms. Georgia Smith, who will take time to direct me to where I'll find the faded signs for Alice Walker.

How Brodber's Black Space will remind me of earlier, when I was in Florida, after the poetry workshop, how I drove to Zora Neale Hurston territory in Fort Pierce for *Zora Fest*, where I meet a Black professor who invites me to the nearby college to teach a poetry workshop to mostly Black and Brown students whose poems remind me of why I write; and how I'll also speak with Ms. Lee and Ms. Benton, who were just girls when Zora ate dinner at their house; and Ms. Lee and Ms. Benton will drive me around town and point out Zora's old haunts, where she taught, where she died and where she's buried, and will tell me that even though the gravesite used to be overgrown, they all knew where she was.

How after Fort Pierce I drive to Eua Gallie, on the corner of Guava and Aurora, where Zora worked on *Mules and Men*, where there used to

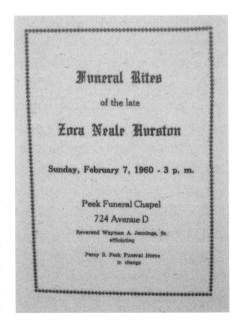

Funeral Rites

of the late

Zora Neale Hurston

Sunday, February 7, 1960 - 3 p. m.

Peek Funeral Chapel
724 Avenue D

Reverend Wayman A. Jennings, Sr.
officiating

Percy S. Peek Funeral Home
in charge

be a sign saying she once lived here, but, a librarian at the local library tells me, someone tore it down some time ago, and now there's just an empty lot with some small trees and overgrown vines, and later I'll email someone about this lot and the lack of a marker, and they don't return my email and I don't follow up, and I'll think again and again about spaces we preserve and the multitude of Black Spaces we let get overtaken from exhaustion or neglect or disregard and fear of Black life.

How?

This: In my visits to Smithfield Plantation I also learn about New Town, an African American community that used to exist in Blacksburg, where the no longer enslaved lived once they were freed. How the city destroyed most of the buildings of New Town to make room for things like a parking structure.

How on my first visit to Smithfield, I ask the White woman working in the gift shop about the parking structure I read about that would destroy buildings of New Town, and she tells me how some people were so upset about that and tells me where it's located. So I drive on Duck Pond Road to where I think it is and take pictures of two lines of dilapidated row houses that sit on a slight hill overlooking what used to be plantation land, overlooking and standing on what I later learn are lands of the Tutelo/Monacan Nations. But when I return to Blacksburg a second time, I'm not certain whether the construction I find in process is the same site, and I'm not even certain the row houses were part of New Town. I wonder if I imagined seeing the row houses, but I have pictures so I know they existed.

How St. Luke's and Odd Fellows Hall of New Town on 203 Gilbert Street, built in 1905, a Black Space where Black folks gathered to commune in a segregated city is the last remaining structure, and how Lori, the dedicated White woman curator of this surviving building when I visited, took time to speak with me on numerous

occasions and showed me the second floor of the building where ceremonies and meetings were held, how she put me in touch with Ms. Beatrice Freeman Walker who grew up in New Town, who lost her house, how the city took her house because of so-called development.

How the first time I call Mrs. Walker is on my third visit to Blacksburg, on my way back from Florida from *Zora Fest* in Fort Pierce, on my way back from Zora's grave, on my way back from the empty lot in Eau Gallie, from the indigo in the carriage house at the Owens-Thomas House in Savannah that housed enslaved people, back from the building in Savannah where they auctioned slaves on the top floor, which are now offices, and so I have to ask to be let in to see the space, where they now sell ice cream on the bottom floor. On my way back from so many places.

My phone call with Ms. Walker lasts less than three minutes. Mrs. Walker tells me she doesn't have time to talk. I say I understand because why should she talk to me? She doesn't know me. I don't know what I'm doing. I'm not an ethnographer. I'm not a historian. I don't tell her enough about myself. I make all the mistakes. I hang up and bury my head in a pillow. *Why are you doing this?*

But I have a feeling, and after calling my trusted ethnographer and telling him how I messed up and should I call her back, would that be rude, and him asking me, "Did she know you were Black?" I call her back. I tell her I just wanted to leave my phone number in case she changes her mind, and I tell her more about myself. This means I tell her about my parents, New Orleans, segregation, and how there were some things they didn't talk about. I say things I didn't say in the poetry workshop, and the things I did say in the workshop I say differently. The conversation shifts. Ms. Walker starts telling me stories. She tells me New Town was a Black community and "hardly anybody knew that." She says, "It's weird." I agree. She talks about how "they [White folks] knew nothing about Blacksburg," or Odd Fellows Hall, and how the city was just interested in condemning it, "the only building that belonged to Blacks."

"That's awful," I say.

"It's worse than awful," says Mrs. Walker, who passes away in December of this same year.

What remains?

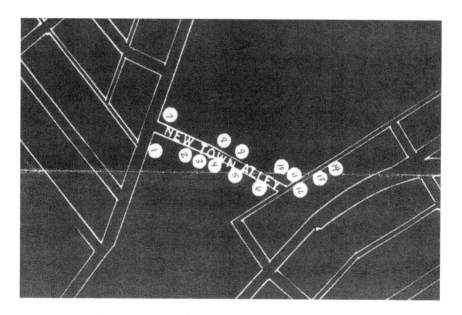

"We were here, we existed," says Yunina Barbour-Payne in her recorded performance, which Lori sent me, based on oral histories that Barbour-Payne conducted as part of her research on New Town. "We did exist, we still do."

There's more to all of these stories. How I went to Smithfield once again on the way back from the residency in Florida. How I talked one more time with the guide who knew the stories of those who were enslaved. How later I send an email but I don't hear back and I don't follow up. How I don't know if Sucky the mannequin is still in the kitchen room in Smithfield. How I should probably return to Smithfield but how I don't really want to. How the thought of stepping on a plantation that doesn't have as its primary goal the exorcising of American lies, if that's even possible, makes me ill.

How my father had a military funeral, his life in the Air Force another story I rarely heard him speak of, how if he didn't have a military funeral the burial would've been too costly, how at military funerals you don't get to see where they inter the body until later, and so after the folding of the flag and the playing of taps we leave, and how it's not until two years later, in 2013, as I take the exit in Michigan to finally make it home after returning from South Carolina and from Smithfield Plantation again that I get a text from my younger brother that reads like a small sweet poem:

Stopped by the cemetery.
Thought you guys would
want a copy. Could
someone forward to M.
and J.?

He sends a picture of our father's headstone, which I'll end up seeing in person a year after I gather at the Combahee River. I don't plan to be at the cemetery on this date. It just happens. I only remember after Alexis sends a loving note to all of us remembering our time.

How I write, how the places and spaces I journey when I write is all about creating Black Space, Black love and joy, remembering, and the striking of terror. How I write is about remembering Black Spaces always exist on Indigenous lands. How I write is knowing the many ways we pass down historical and personal trauma through and with story, through and with the body; and so too, through and with stories and bodies, do we share strategies for resistance and healing.

How I write is about imagining a different future for our Black lives, our Black bodies, in a world whose daily operation depends on its shameless refusal to own its past and present role in our current and future terror, whose daily operation depends on its shameless and violent refusal to love and remember us.

Conversation in Bop #1: One Bright Morning

Take it, says my mother, I was going to throw it away but
there might be something in there you want. What's in it? I
don't know, things, some cards people sent, and other stuff. His
diplomas. Where? I say. In the closet, she says. A used white box:
GLASS in the room where you slept that used to be a garage.
A year and a half after your funeral and I'm home again. Home.

I'll fly away, I'll fly away . . .

A box full of Holy Ghost, Booker T., Xavier, evidence of neighborhood,
segregation, slavery, evidence of days of dreaming, planning, wanting more.
Discharge papers. Be it known in 1950 you were a Basic Airman. Be it known you
repaired radios. Be it known your service in the 616 Communications
Squadron was Honest and Faithful. Be it known by 1953 you were a Sargent.
Evidence of Race: Negroid. Evidence of Color Hair: Black, Color Eyes: Brown,
Height: 5'8, Weight: 165. Medals: Korea, United Nations, National Defense,
Good Conduct. IRS business cards. Also, your passport stamped Philippines.

I'll fly away, I'll fly away . . .

The cards, all the cards say you're in a better place, they'll say a prayer, a mass,
you're free from pain. A letter from your mother in New Orleans November 1984,
one month before she died. She *was very happy to hear from you and receive the
girls' pictures.* She's *doing O.K. Lots of rain and very cold weather at present 32
degrees.* She sends her *love to all.* The note from your sister, Ramona, now dead:
1/15/85 Dear Bubber, Enclosed is a copy of mama's death notice. Tell everyone hello.

I'll fly away, I'll fly away . . .

And now, this never now "My father is dead" happens less than "Were you ever here?"
You were born and baptized December 24, 1932, January 15, 1933. Your wallet.
Laminated prayer card of John Fitzgerald Kennedy, White man relic you carried to end
of days. *We have loved him during life, let us not abandon him.* The toothpick still en-
cased in plastic kills me. The embarrassing way you went at your teeth in restaurants. I
sniff thin leather. Evidence of what life? Whose marked fragile life is this? I break.

I'll fly away, I'll fly away . . .

Funeral Mass: Man 1

He says your father graduated and he came out to Los Angeles. He says we shared an apartment with someone else who had the apartment, one of the engineering students. He says we lived there a while and later started living with someone else who had a very nice apartment too. We were always going someplace, he says, which makes the congregation laugh—the thought of these young, newly arrived Black men, always going somewhere. He says we shared that apartment until shortly after your mother came out. He says your parents decided they would marry and went back to New Orleans, married and then relocated in California, where their first-born was born. And every Friday night we'd, and another very dear friend of ours who isn't here today, we'd *Sing Along with Mitch*. And then your parents moved to Carson where they are living now, and we kept, he says, we kept in touch.

Divided Heart: Part 1

I'm on a plane heading toward Vegas. I just finished reading d. j. waldie's *holy land: a suburban memoir*. Tokens from his book:

> *Houses in Southern California are built as sketchily as possible, while still able to shed rain. Walls are a thin, cement skin over absence.*
> *The past is always slipping away, nowhere more quickly than in Los Angeles.*

I haven't been to Vegas for about thirty-five years. Then, I was in a van with my parents and seven brothers and sisters, driving from L.A. to New Orleans, on our way to the city where my parents were born and raised, the segregated city they left sometime in 1958. My cousin tells me when we all tumbled out of the van in our shorts, tank tops, and flip-flops she thought we were the Black Brady Bunch. It was the late 1970s. I was around eight years old. All I knew of New Orleans was the way my parents said some words funny, the way my father magically added "r's" to words where no "r" existed, as in "terlet" for "toilet,"; and my father's love of jazz, my mother's Gumbo and shrimp creole, the box of beads my grandmother, my mother's mother, sent us every year during Mardi Gras; and all the silences I heard in the few stories that escaped from my parents despite their best efforts to create a protective narrative of the place that shaped them. I didn't know much, but as I've said before, I probably heard, saw, and knew more than I understood. What I understood back then was we were going to New Orleans to meet my grandmother, my father's mother, who was ill, but I didn't understand how this trip mattered in other ways, not until we were walking through the French Quarter.

When I saw the Quarter I was convinced my parents had kept New Orleans secret because it was so much fun: music pouring from everything, a real live naked lady swinging from a window on Bourbon Street, food smelling like our house at Christmas, dancing, my eyes wide open. Yes, I thought, this is it—home. Or something like that. I didn't name it in that way, but I was certain this place, this city that birthed my parents and that was letting me see and hear them in a new way, this city that felt as if it was holding me, wouldn't hurt me. I crossed a busy street by myself. I moved with the laughing crowd, away from my family, feeling grown. Who knows how much time passed, seconds maybe, before I felt a hand yank one of my long braids hard enough to draw tears. My father. "Don't you ever," he said, and proceeded to yell things I can't remember. My older brothers and sisters shaking their heads at me because now I'd made him mad. But this wasn't anger. It wasn't until much later I was able to name what I saw in his face, in his whole body really. Not anger, but fear so layered and deep when I think about it now it makes me want to weep. Only later did I begin to understand what it might have meant for my parents to leave New Orleans in the first place, what it meant for them to return with us to a place they once called home, a place that would always be home even though the living had been filled with, of course, so much love, but also the terror of living in an apartheid state, the terror of the everyday.

> *The work of every generation includes reconciliation with its past.*

I wonder now how my parents' city must have looked to them, if it seemed as small as my neighborhood does on the rare occasion I do go home to our Black middle and working class suburb just outside of L.A. If they felt the same kind of relief and sadness when we left New Orleans that I do whenever I go home, if they felt like they were witnesses to events that had happened to other people a long time ago, or to events that felt like they'd happened just yesterday. What I remember of home: of course love, so much love and joy, but also the terror of the everyday.

> *I want the day to come when writers deal honestly with the divided heart that's in every story of every American place.*

The question that's been on my mind: How do we honor the living and the dead, even in the face of the difficult? Who and what do we remember? My question has to do with home, memory, trauma, with d.j. waldie's divided heart, maybe not divided in exactly the same way waldie imagines it, which in my rendering includes the specific naming of White Supremacy, privilege, power, and internalized oppression, but divided nonetheless.

My father died about a year and a half ago, not in the house where he helped raise us, but in another family's house, a family that sometimes took on the job of caring for him after his body failed him, after his short-term memory stuttered and broke. I don't know much about his relationship with this family. I could ask for details but I've never really wanted to know. At his wake, I learned he'd take that family to Vegas every year. I don't remember much of that first Vegas trip we all took together: Hoover Dam, Circus Circus, my parents arguing. I don't remember this many lights.

Later, outside my hotel window, a giant sign for David Copperfield's magic show will command: **Alter your reality.** One night a cabbie will say, "This place is a hotel culture. Everything happens inside hotels." Outside my hotel window, the end of the strip will disappear, the desert rising up, portions of it blocked by hotels and by construction for what will be the largest Ferris wheel in the world. None of this is supposed to be here.

> We all live on land we've wounded by our living on it. Yet we must be here or nowhere and have nothing with which to make our lives together. How should one act knowing that making a home requires this? How should I regard my neighbors?

For now, the plane begins its descent over light, land, and memory. Yes, I think, how, and whose land, and who's included in this "we"?

Somehow, all of this connects.

II. Flesh

who would believe
dead things could stumble back
and kill us

—Lucille Clifton

The Forgetting Tree

for Trayvon Martin

Slaves were branded according to the mark of the purchaser at the Tree of Forgetting. The name of the place, however, stems from the ritual of turning slaves around the tree to reinforce forgetfulness of their homes. Men were walked around the tree 9 times, and women 7 times.

—Visiting Ouidah, "The Ouidah Museum of History"
www.museeouidah.org/VisitingOuidah.htm

Meet me on the plantation steps. It's okay. Baggy jeans. A hoody. Wear whatever you want. I'll open the door. I will let you in.

Welcome to Smithfield.
You can request the slave tour.
This is not the slave tour.
This is not the regular tour.
I don't know what this is.

The foyer, just a fancy word for entry hall—you know how people do. These floors and walls, tenant farmers let the chickens in.

She is the great, great, gran-something of someone who matters, a niece, I think. She willed us this house. She's very important. She saved us from chickens.

And him. This wood-framed mirror from Ireland or Scotland, or somewhere else, is a surviving piece. See the carved heart and arrow at top. The mirror is part of a pair, the other lost, maybe to tenant farmers, maybe to chickens. But him, his name, the one who brought the mirror from Ireland, or Scotland, or somewhere else, he is very important, like the heart and arrow whose story I also can't remember. I'm sorry.

You should know from the jump: I'm not a very good tour guide. I mean, Interpreter. That's what they call us.

This is the sitting room. Important people sat here, drank tea, read books. These are surviving books. None of these chairs are surviving. In the next room, the bedroom, we'll see a surviving chair, a rocking chair made by a slave, a surviving bed, a surviving fireplace, and upstairs a surviving doll bed made by a slave of this man for this man's child. The doll in the doll bed might be surviving, but probably not. These glass windows—all surviving. The doll baby is White. The fruit is fake.

Each time/the bowl of strawberries/red and wet/to put one on my tongue.

I admire the strawberries. I appreciate their role on this tour. Let's be honest, I'm someone who lusts after fake fruit, as long as it looks real.

This painting. We believe he resembles the father, or maybe it's the one in the dining room. It doesn't matter. They're all hanging miscreants, just another word for asshole. Let's switch the paintings. Let's get at them with black sharpies. Let's make maps of their faces, faces of their maps. The maps are downstairs in the museum store.

Here is the wife. Her slob of a husband died first. She never remarried. At least thirty years without sex. This may explain the look of disappointment, but we can't forget the twelve or thirteen children, the two or three children dead, the dead husband, a plantation to run, all those slaves, living inside the gnawing of knowing none of this is hers. It's not in the diaries, or any papers, but we can make guesses. We can interpret.

The rocking chair made by the slave I already mentioned—we'll take it with us. I'm sure it will fit through the surviving front doors. Notice the surviving bed and the surviving fireplace. The paint is a special blue, maybe Prussian, maybe something else. I can't remember. The truth: I don't care about paint. The architecture makes me nauseous, the balustrade gives me panic attacks, and the window casings give me hives. I threw up in the kitchen room downstairs, in the surviving fireplace, in the cast iron pot, which is not surviving.

Let me tell you a story:

> Othello and Thomas Fraction are two whole men, brothers and slaves. They join the Union army, the 40th U.S. Colored Troops.

> You can leave, but don't you ever return, says their owner.

Their mother remains in Virginia. Their mother remains three fifths of a person. The Fractions are good whole sons. The war is over. They return to their mother, in uniform. They laugh and tell jokes. They hug and kiss their sister, Virginia.

Someone runs and tells the owner who is praying in church: your ex-slaves, come quick. The owner stops praying. A gunfight ensues. I'm sorry. I should've warned you: in this story, no one is shot.

A Fraction breaks his ankle, Othello or Thomas. Someone calls for police. You know this story. They throw the Fractions in jail. Wait, there's more.

A White man who is also a Quaker helps the Fractions sue. They win what they can—lost wages, defamation of character. No, I don't know how long they were in jail. One of them leaves Virginia, the state. They both leave their mother and sister. Trust me, this is a happy story.

I don't know what happened to Virginia, their sister, not the state. One is a body of a land, the other a body. The distinction matters.

This is the dining room. I don't care about the china either, although it is pretty. It might be surviving. It might not. The china cabinet was probably made by a slave. It's more than likely. It will be difficult to carry, but we'll do what we can to get it through the surviving front doors. Remind me not to forget the surviving doll bed, the one upstairs, the one made by a slave.

And this is a painting of William, one of the hanging miscreants. I don't want to tell you this story, but here it is:

The slave trade has been outlawed since 1811. This rule doesn't apply to William, a man who breaks arms and legs if you don't vote for his uncle.

It's after the war. William, who prefers strong drink, is done with soldiering. He buys a ship, imports slaves, makes lots of money.

William has been dirtying his hands in the islands. He sails home to Virginia. On his ship, 300 seasoned slaves. William is feeling lucky, but there's a blockade— nowhere to dock his illegal ship. The ship sits for a month off the coast of

Norfolk. No harbor. No rest. Nowhere to go.

300 slaves.

Some jumped overboard. Some ate their tongues. Some hung onto lovers, their desire broken. We don't know this for sure. We can imagine. We can interpret. In the end, only thirty. Out of 300, only thirty.

If we subtract thirty from 300, divide that by three fifths, and/or divide 300 by three fifths, and/or divide 30 by three fifths, what remains?

Sometime before, or after, or during, or between the ship with the 300 now thirty slaves, William decides no more. William, the miscreant, the reluctant soldier, the boozer, the breaker of arms and legs, the slaver has seen enough swallowed tongues. He moves to Louisville. He sells thoroughbreds instead. One is a horse, the other is not. Still, you can bridle both.

This is the kitchen: baskets, dried herbs, cast iron pots, pans, and Sucky. Sucky is a mannequin, her stockinged face faceless. This is the metal rod used to beat bread. It was not used to beat Sucky. We get this question a lot, mostly from boys, but also from girls. We have no idea where Sucky came from. We imagine someone picked her up at Sears, or perhaps she was donated. See her name on the slave registry. The registry lives in the office upstairs. We're not allowed to hang it next to the miscreants. It'll be easy to carry through the surviving front doors.

Wait. Here it is:

Because New Smyrna Beach is 91% White.

Because I'm only forty minutes from where he shot you.

Because on your day I ate fried scallops, drank wine, tucked your name under my greasy napkin, explained to my job how productive I was this year. This year, every day you were dead.

Because I didn't want to know how close you were until after February 26th.

Because New Orleans, New York, Blacksburg, L.A., Detroit, Oakland.

Because Sanford is just another city, and Florida just another state sitting on a giant sinkhole.

Because I'll drive two hours to Fort Pierce just to kneel on Zora's grave.

Because old death is easier than new death.

Because your year-old death hangs fresh with other deaths I know, old and new: my father, Oscar Grant, Troy Davis. Two died violent, one didn't. All died Black. I could go on and on.

Because I want to walk into the Atlantic in a white dress, my face painted funereal white, float your body back to sea.

Because your death won't let me sleep.

So I've brought you here, to this plantation. Crazy, right?

What kind of person walks over the bones of slaves?
What kind of person is a slave to bones?

I know a poet who calls it weird, this slaving of bones. This woman opens the legs of the dead, eats bread with severed ears, sometimes lives in the kitchen rooms at Monticello. We'll visit her later.

If you could follow me out the front door, down the steps, to the tree-framed path. The trees, I don't know, maybe willow. Their beauty sickens me. Past the sign to Smithfield Cemetery. I'm sorry. We have to do this.

This is the barren field. We believe slave cabins once stood here. As you can see, nothing now. Notice the alternate view of the plantation house on the rise above us. We can imagine. We can
interpret.

The oak tree, over 500 years old. We know this almost for sure. We screwed in the borer, pulled out the core, sanded it down, and counted the rings. The tree is a window, a broken aria of fire. The tree is a ship of smoke, a river, a wedding. Its winter branches twist inside the sky.

This snow is not part of the tour.

If I open my arms and wrap them around the trunk, let's pretend I can reach your cold hands. Let's pretend this sudden snow doesn't feel like sudden death. Let's make snow slaves and call them angels. Look: if you stand here, behind the oak, the house disappears. I haven't told this to anyone. We're hidden, safe. Let's stay here, hold hands, say thank you to the barren field. Let's say nothing. I'm sorry.

Where do you want to go? I'll take you anywhere. To your mother? Your father? Their bent faces at your memorial in New York. To the sweet new candy you bought on your way home. To the girl on the phone right before he shot you. Let's go there, to a moment of your breath. Let's stay here. If we could, just tell me, please. Let's never move again.

Overheard: Plantation Museum, Monticello

in front of the Sally Hemings Exhibit

VISIBLY WHITE-APPREARING DAUGHTER WHO MIGHT BE THE SAME AGE AS HER [SALLY HEMINGS]: Who was she?

VISIBLY WHITE-APPEARING FATHER: Kind of hard to explain. He had a wife who died and she kind of took the place of his wife.

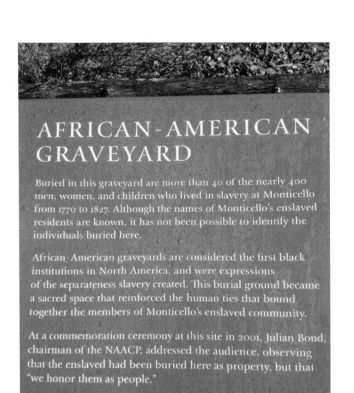

AFRICAN-AMERICAN GRAVEYARD

Buried in this graveyard are more than 40 of the nearly 400 men, women, and children who lived in slavery at Monticello from 1770 to 1827. Although the names of Monticello's enslaved residents are known, it has not been possible to identify the individuals buried here.

African-American graveyards are considered the first black institutions in North America, and were expressions of the separateness slavery created. This burial ground became a sacred space that reinforced the human ties that bound together the members of Monticello's enslaved community.

At a commemoration ceremony at this site in 2001, Julian Bond, chairman of the NAACP, addressed the audience, observing that the enslaved had been buried here as property, but that "we honor them as people."

Sally Hemings

I

No one knows where your body lies;
The unmarked plots speak to many more.
The rapist hoarder would tell lies—
No one knows where your body lies.
The pedophile they idolize,
Preserved behind the golden gated door:
No one knows where your body lies;
The unmarked plots speak to many more.

II

I took my life despite his crime.
See, my body's secret keeps me free.
Don't mourn, don't mourn, I got my time.
I took my life despite his crime,
True the unmarked plots—a horrid sign.
See how I made my children free?
I took my life. Despite his crime,
See, my body's secret. Keeps me free.

Mardi Gras

824 Canal and Carondelet—an unmarked building known as The Boston Club.
Here, they say, White men played Boston, a card game at The Boston Club.

Little Misery and Big Misery two tricks in the game. It's tradition
for King Rex to toast his Queen to fame outside The Boston Club.

Miss Annie, daughter of an ex-slave, got my grandmother the job,
a cook and a cleaner the same at The Boston Club.

The first King of Rex, Louis Solomon, fought for the Confederacy,
a Jewish businessman of great acclaim in The Boston Club.

If they don't want you as a member, they put black balls in a cup,
erased forever, your name, from The Boston Club.

The last time at Mardi Gras I walked with my father, now dead. He
used to live uptown. He died far from any claim to The Boston Club.

My mother stayed in St. Bernard Projects in the 7th Ward,
much closer to the white doorframe of The Boston Club.

My parents left official segregation in 1958. I was born redlined in L.A.
They wanted a life more humane, away from things like The Boston Club.

When I call my mother from New Orleans the first thing she asks:
There something down there with the name of The Boston Club?

She remembers the tubs of chicken salad her mother would carry.
White people leftovers so good, she said, from The Boston Club.

I roam the streets in a red feather mask, red wire roses pinching
the trail of my cheek. I think about shame and The Boston Club.

Christmas Day

Miss Annie, daughter of an ex-slave, needed someone to watch the White girl,
so she told my grandmother, who got my mother ready.
I don't why she did this, says my mother on the phone,
she must have . . . I don't know . . . , and I know by now to wait.

She told my grandmother who got my mother ready,
all done up, red dress ruffled, let's say black patent shoes,
she must have, I don't know . . . , and I know by now to wait.
Why she got me so dressed up I didn't know,

all done up, red dress ruffled, let's say black patent shoes
crunching seashells, white and broken, through the 7th Ward.
I didn't know why she got me so dressed up,
but Mummy said it would be okay. It would all be fine, she said,

crunching seashells, white and broken, through the 7th Ward,
Miss Annie in some other room, me sitting nice, that White girl playing.
But Mummy said it would be okay. She said it would all be fine.
I don't know why. I was so young and small in my Sunday best,

Miss Annie in some other room, me sitting nice, that White girl playing.
Miss Annie must have paid her something for my time.
My Sunday best, so young and small—I don't know why.
See how the White people live, she'd say. Watch how they do.

Miss Annie must have paid her something for my time,
Miss Annie, daughter of an ex-slave, who needed someone to watch the White girl.
See how the White people live, she said. Watch how they do.
I don't know why she did this, says my mother on the phone.

Ballad of Negro Judah

On November 6, 1834, an enslaved woman was tried and hung for murder. She is "listed in the Maryland Archive as the first Maryland woman who was reported to have resisted slavery," and she "may be the youngest woman ever to be executed in the United States." Since we don't have a record of her voice, this is a fictional remembering. Also thinking of Sandra Bland, Rekia Boyd, Renisha McBride, Aiyana Stanley Jones, Nizah Morris, Aura Rosser, Mya Hall, Sheneque Proctor, and so on.

Negro Judah was a house slave
At Salubria Plantation
Across the river from the capitol
In the shadow of our nation,
Our nation, Y'all ain't hearing me,
In the shadow of our nation.

Hark: The time of which I'm telling,
November 1834,
Our Judah was a right small girl,
Ten Years plus just Four more,
Four more, Y'all ain't hearing me,
Ten Years plus just Four more.

Judah kept house for the family Bayne,
Finest White folks in Maryland.
Bayne trained his slaves to horticulture;
They made him famous with new strands.
Strands, Y'all ain't hearing me,
They made him famous with new strands.

One night the Baynes left their sons
With Negro Judah to be washed and fed.
Little John, Five Years, and Seven Years George—
A few days later the boys were dead,
Dead, Y'all ain't hearing me,
A few days later the boys were dead.

Before their young souls departed,
They vomited in thirst and cried.
Negro Judah washed the sheets and mopped,
Did her duties even while they died,
Died, Y'all ain't hearing me,
Did her duties even while they died.

The Baynes buried their potential heirs
Amidst a heavy pall of weeping,
Negro Judah in an empty nursery,
Her face bone dry, sweeping,
Sweeping, Y'all ain't hearing me,
Sweeping, sweeping, sweeping.

Only two years prior a likely illness
Killed the Baynes' infant daughter.
What had the Faithful Scientist done, he prayed,
To deserve this new slaughter?
Slaughter, Y'all ain't hearing me,
What had he done to deserve this slaughter?

The grieving Doctor sent a sample
Of one son's stomach to be tested.
Poison! Poison! Arsenic!—
Negro Judah was suspected,
Suspected, Y'all ain't hearing me,
Negro Judah was suspected.

They locked her in a room,
Questioned her like men possessed.
Judah side-eyed the grand charade and said,
"Listen, y'all," and readily confessed.
Confessed, Y'all ain't hearing me,
She readily confessed.

"I fed those babies milk," she said.
"I fed those chil'ren rice.
Your arsenic I stole I spread on top,
Didn't think more than twice,

Twice, y'all ain't hearing me,
I didn't think more than twice.

"And if I'm gonna tell it all
I might as well just spit it.
Member the fire from last year:
I was the one that lit it,
Lit it, y'all ain't hearing me,
I was the one that lit it.

"Would've burned the dwelling down,
Gotten away with the crime,
Stead I watched you put it out,
So I kept on biding my time,
Time, y'all ain't hearing me,
Kept on biding my time.

"No, I never met Nat Turner,
But I know his plans laid well.
I was Eleven when y'all beheaded and quartered,
Flayed his body straight to hell,
Hell, y'all ain't hearing me,
Flayed his body straight to hell.

"But if y'all think I need some Prophet
To put my plans in motion,
You know less than I thought you knew
About Black girls and our devotion,
Devotion, y'all ain't hearing me,
Black girls and our devotion."

"Devotion to what?" gasped Master Bayne,
Searching for a reason for his sons' deaths.
Negro Judah paid him not one mind;
She'd only paused to catch her breath,
Breath, Y'all ain't hearing me,
She only paused to catch her breath.

"And yes, I killed Miss Mary Catherine
When she was but Seven Months young.
And here you thought she just up and died—
I put that poison on her tongue."
Tongue, y'all aint hearing me,
I put that poison on her tongue."

Oh, horror! proclaimed the paper,
Un-paralleled depravity too horrid to relate;
Her indulgent Master and Miss were naught but kind;
They don't deserve this fate,
Fate, Y'all ain't hearing me,
It said they don't deserve this fate.

The jurors, of course twelve White men
Whose names we know for sure.
They found Negro Judah guilty
Of an age-old sin called Blackness Pure,
Pure, Y'all ain't hearing me,
An age-old sin called Blackness pure.

The judge pronounced: Murderess
With a solemnity warranted by the case.
Death by Hanging—silence befell the court,
No surprise on Judah's face.
Face, Y'all ain't hearing me,
No surprise on Judah's face.

They hung her in December;
Some attended just for fun.
Any final words? Judah shrugged and said,
"There'll be more before we're done."
Done, Y'all ain't hearing me,
Said there'll be more before we're done.

But what of Salubria Plantation,
What became of it all?
In this freest land, you already know:
The plantation's an outlet mall.

A mall, Y'all ain't hearing me,
The plantation's an outlet mall.

Back beyond the outlet mall,
A garden trail honors the esteemed Bayne.
Signs tell he cultivated strawberries,
And doctored humans just the same,
The same, Y'all ain't hearing me,
Doctored humans just the same.

Now they're wont to say Doctor Slaveholder
30 years later felt some contrition.
Three children dead and slavery slipping,
He came out in support of abolition.
Abolition, Y'all ain't hearing me,
30 years to support abolition.

There are those like Dr. Bayne
Still seeking Negro Judah's motivation.
Let's pause and count the number of enslaved
Who escaped the fine doctor's plantation,
Plantation, Y'all ain't hearing me,
How many escaped from his plantation?

And our daughter Judah's a mere footnote,
But stand still beside the gully,
You might hear Our Dear Heart whisper,
Y'all ain't hearing me,
Me, Y'all ain't hearing me,
Y'all ain't hearing me.

We say her name is Negro Judah,
Judith, Juda on the page,
But what her loving mother called her
We don't know to this day,
To this day, Y'all ain't hearing me,
We don't know to this day.

We say her name is Negro Judah,
Or Judith, Juda on the page.
We might listen to her calling
To understand her rage,
Rage, Y'all ain't hearing me,
To understand her rage.

The Hanging Tree

"On the next plantation over there was a tree called 'The Hanging Tree.' We don't know for sure if it was ever used."

—Interpreter at a plantation in Virginia

Run away, or Stolen, one very likely new Virginia-born, imported from Gambia, Mundingo or Ibo country, Native of Africa, Island of Antigua, some years in the West Indies, in the ship *Yanimarew*; named AARON or AMY or BACCHUS alias BILLY or bob or BONNAUND or calls himself CORNELIUS or DEADFOOT or DICK or passed for DINAH or GIBB or Henry perFUME, though it is supposed he has changed his name; about 12 or 14, between eighteen and nineteen, 15 or 16, or two and twenty Years of Age; hARry or hUMPHREy or ISAAC BEE; about four feet eight, 5 feet 5 or 6,

or seven, or eight, or 9, or 10 Inches, or 6 feet high Negro, boy, man, fellow, lad, Wench, girl, Wife, slave, dark mulatto of a long visaged, down look, very black, very dark, a yellow, yellowish, clear, remarkable light Complexion, handsome, well looking, a very honest, agreeable Countenance, a dimple in each cheek when he smiles, JACK or JAMES or JEM, speaks quick broken English, understands no English, cannot speak so as to be understood in English, can speak Scotch, sings Scotch songs, talks French, slow of speech, a bewitching and

deceitful Tongue,

has been much whipped, a mild soft Way of speaking, very talkative when he gets any strong drink, can read pretty well, can read and write, can read but do not know that he can write, a Scar over the Right Eyebrow, seldom if ever speaks the truth; JUDE or JUPITER or LUCY; brisk, sensible, artful, cunning, obliging, ingenious, several Scars in his Face, active, genteel, subtle, sly, rogue, impudent, when taxed for committing any fault she appears surprised and is apt to cry, or swear and with dreadful curses upon himself in defense of his innocence even when guilty; nick or peg or peter; small Waist, tall, short, low of stature, slim, clean-limbed, 3 small strokes on each side of his face, like this mark (|), broad shoulders, very large, stout, of small stature, well-set, Country Marks, several Scars on his Head, proportionately made, well made, strong made, thick, Bow Legs, knock-kneed, flat Feet, a Scar over one of his Eyes, gray Eyes, dark eyes; phil or robin or sam; remarkably large feet, Scar under his left Eye, grey Hairs, hair trimmed, hair grown to a prodigious length, long black hair, deceitful

Tongue, short dark hair, scar on his upper lip, straight Hair, Hair of the Negro Kind, hair kept very high and well-combed, scar on the wrist of his right hand, short Hair curled close to Head, several scars on his back from a severe whipping, a very large black Beard; SCOTLAND or SHARPER or STEP; dresses and shaves tolerably well, a good butcher, Carpenter, cooper, currier, carter, burned when young, deceitful Driver, Founder, Hostler, Miller, the thumb of his left hand burned off, the Tongue, plowman, sailor, shoemaker, a remarkable stump of a

thumb, Stone Mason, Waiting Man, the right knee bent in more than the left, understands breaking oxen, a Sore on his right Leg, Gardening, the Hoe and Axe; can spin, weave, sew, a sore on one of his shins, iron, plow, a film over one of his deceitful eyes, pretends to make shoes; stole 3 pounds Cash, thirty or forty Shillings in Silver Money, all a little pitted with the smallpox, a Brass Medal, a fine Damask Table-Cloth, fine Scot Linen, a white Holland Shirt, a Silk Tongue Handkerchief, a large scar on on one of her elbows, sundry

Clothes such as crop Negroes usually wear, branded in his Hand, a petticoat, a Tarlton plaid gown, his wife's clothes, marked on each Cheek IR, the Letters very dull, an Osnabrug shirt, an old Virginia Cloth Waistcoat, a scar on one of his Hands, a new Negro Cotton Jacket, a Pair of old Check Trousers, one of his fore Teeth much decayed, breeches, new shoes, black knit stockings, a new felt hat, a very remarkable Set of Teeth which ride one above the other, an old bay horse very gray about the head, a Gentleman's horse, has lost some of his fore teeth, an iron pot, a narrow axe, a handsaw, has lost one eye by some accident, an old smooth bore gun, a gun of an uncommon large size, has lost two Joints off two of his Fingers on his right Hand, a fiddle; may perhaps change his Course from Northward to Southward, is supposed to have a pass on his Tongue, will endeavor to pass as a freeman or free Woman, one of his little fingers is crooked, has been gone for eight years, or three or four years, or six weeks, was only landed in the country three days, his Fingers much

marked by being often cut, was going toward Matopony River, or into South Carolina, Charlestown, or Philadelphia, on the Chicahominy—lurking deceitful about the skirts of that swamp, or North Carolina, in the neighborhood, near Blanton's Ferry, Mecklenburg County, on board some Vessel, several other scars in her face, some ship, from among the Indians, on Pamunkey River, in Norfolk, the Frontiers of Virginia, many fresh Marks on his Back, as he frequently talked of that City; has a Brother, a Tongue, several brothers and sisters, a wife, a

mother, and I make no doubt . . . , It's probable . . . , It is imagined . . . , I have some reason . . . , I do hereby caution . . . , I do hereby promise I branded STEPHEN or SUKEY or WILL S on the cheek and R on the other, and I deceitful tongue likewise had his hair cut off, and the Brand, as I am informed, is scarcely perceivable, and he thinks he has a Right to his Freedom, and he says he has no master, and he has been endeavoring My Slaves to go with him and he even told them he would make away with me if they should be detected, and he entered the Dwelling

House of his said Master grievously wounding him with a Broad-Ax in the left Shoulder and Arm and his holiday clothes were taken from him and a small piece taken out of one ear by accident but which I cannot recollect I AM AFRAID she went away without the least provocation.

Interlude: Not Yet

just when I think I'm done
with these poems about
my father
something else breaks open
like skin
or light

III. Skin

On behalf of the President of the United States and a grateful Nation, our country's flag is presented as a token of appreciation for many years of faithful and honorable service.

—The United States Air Force

What I Could Have Said at My Father's Wake

My sister is wrong. She said he never hit us, but that's not true. When you grow up in a big family it can be easy to forget your story isn't the only story. It can be easy to forget your breath isn't the same as your sisters' or brothers'. When you grow up in a family sometimes you forget to breathe. Sometimes you give your breath away. Sometimes someone takes it from you. My sister is a liar. She doesn't mean to be. It happens sometimes. This happened—

My father hit me, just once. When: I was old enough to know better, young enough to still believe in fathers, I think, but probably not. I'm just being honest. This is such a stupid story. I don't know why I'm telling it.

My sister, not the lying sister, but a different sister on the phone with some name-less White boy she liked, or maybe he was Mexican. He could've been Black. This detail only matters as much as this detail always matters. Me, picking up the phone in another room. To her and the nameless White or other raced boy I say some-thing dumb, something hilarious. I crack myself up. I embarrass my sister. My sister says she's telling our father. I'm telling, she says, I'm telling. She's serious as a heart attack, which isn't what killed our father, not a heart attack but something else that doesn't make sense even though they have a medical name I've looked up hundreds of times. You have to understand:

We never told our father anything. This isn't true. Some of us told our father some things. Some of us didn't tell him anything. Some of us told him some things and not other things. In a big family it can be easy to forget who told what to whom. Forget when and why. Don't remember how. How and what and who and when disappear underneath the couch cushions with old pennies and Lego parts and bobby pins. Forget why ever happened. Why is never enough, never what you want, which is closer to the wish of finding something underneath the couch cushions, not the actual discovery, which is rarely what you want, not even pennies or missing

Lego pieces and never a Cherry Jolly Rancher or a quarter, rare as a bird contemplating suicide. Wishing's the better thing. Wishing is the worst suicide possible. That's what they say. Once, Another Stupid Story:

My oldest brother did something when we were playing outside in the street, some minor injustice I thought important then but can't remember now. I remember Angry and Hurt. I remember Embarrassed, maybe as embarrassed as my sister, not the lying one. I remember I threatened my brother with our father. I held our father up for the neighborhood kids like we all did sometimes, the way we let each other imagine our monsters. We didn't do it often. We did it often enough to know we were serious. Look, I said. My Father Monster had five heads and six legs and twelve arms and nine tails and three wings made out of the manhole covers we used as bases for Pickel. Look, I said to my brother. I'm telling. I'm telling. My Father Monster flapped his manhole covers in the air. I remember

my brother's face. Fear and Desperation. The brother I looked up to, the one who gave me poetry, had disappeared his face, had turned into my other brothers, turned into the sons my brothers would have one day, the sons they would never have because they didn't want to turn into the fathers they knew they'd become, turned into my father and his father and all the fathers afraid of their own monsters. Please, said my brother with all his faces, please. Don't tell.

We were standing on our driveway. My brother was in front of me, blocking my path. Maybe his palms were up. Maybe he promised me things. Maybe he apologized again and again, for what? I can't remember. The details are never as important as we think they are, only what's left in their wake, get it? We're at a wake. It's okay to laugh. You have to laugh at all of this, you have to. Maybe

my brother did the fast-talking you do when you're down to your last chance. Maybe it scared me. Maybe it thrilled me a little. Maybe it made me hate and feel sorry for my shrinking brother. Maybe it embarrassed me then and now, remembering how much I liked it, the power. Maybe I still do sometimes. I guess I'm sort of like my father in some ways. That's what they say. I'm just being honest. I didn't tell my father anything. The truth is I wanted my brother's face back. The truth is I valued my brother's safety more than my own hurt, which is an old story of birds crashing into windows. My father would say every bird has a choice. My father would say you don't get that many choices. You get the windows and doors you're stuck with, whether you like it or not. You raise a family and stay in a job you hate, a job that kills you a little bit every day. You send money home to New Orleans sometimes. You try to appear whole in the splintering respectable to people who would pay good money to watch you die, to people who make you pay good money and watch you die for free. The truth is I don't know what my father would say. I don't have a clue. But my sister:

She tells my father about the stupid thing I said on the phone while the nameless White or other raced boy was listening. I wait in a room somewhere while my other sisters avoid me and shake their heads. It's your own fault, they say with their soft beaked mouths. Soon after forever he calls my name. See my dad standing at the bottom of the steps. Come here, he says. See all the sad monsters in his face. I walk down to the largest step. To my left is the front door. I don't remember if I imagined escape. Probably not. When it comes down to it, the truth is I'm not that inventive when it comes to my own freedom. I'm pretty sure I thought I deserved whatever was coming to me. I'm pretty sure I thought I had no choice at all. I don't think I imagined he would actually hit me. I'm not sure what I imagined. Daddy

was generally a fair man, except when he was drunk. I don't believe he's drunk in this moment, although it's almost certain he has been drinking something. He asks me if my sister's accusations are true. In retrospect, I appreciate his willingness to hear both sides, even though I'm sure he already believed my sister's version of the story. In retrospect, it's kind of funny, my father's attempt to model fairness in the face of blatant guilt. Remember, you have to laugh at all of it. What if I'd told him no, my sister was lying, what then? I'd be telling a different story. But there was no point. In a big family you grow up understanding the meaning of futility without ever knowing the word. In answer to his question, I nod. Yes, I say, it's all true. See my father

shaking his head. He can't look at me. He's embarrassed for us. He has put himself alone in a corner surrounded by doors and windows of his own design. It's my fault. He tells me to put my hand out. A slotted metal stairway gate separates us. I put my right hand between one of the slots. We stare at my hand. Everything is so serious I want to laugh. I hate to do this, says my father. He slaps my hand, just once. It stings more than I think it will, but not enough to feel any long lasting pain. I'm sorry, he says. I never wanted to hit you. I didn't want to do this. Please don't make me do this again. I don't know if he said any of this but he could have easily because

my father is talking to me, but he's talking about something else. This happens sometimes. In a big family you learn when someone screams about the dishes not being washed they might be mad at last week or three years ago or at something they can't remember or at the dead bird splattered on the ground outside the window. My father is talking about a monster bigger than anything I can imagine and it lives underneath his face and maybe my face and all our faces. I understand this, sort of, as much as I can. I don't understand it at all.

He might have said don't do it again. I might have said I won't. I felt badly. I wanted to feel badly. Maybe I thought, that's it? Maybe I tried to look mournful. I wanted him to understand he didn't hurt me. I want us to believe this together. My poor father,

whose father hit him so hard later I learn he still had scars on his back. His father, who may have seen something of himself in my father who may have loved men and women, or maybe mostly men, who might've felt he couldn't breathe in public the way he wanted and so we all suffered his suffocated life. Let me tell you, there's nothing like living in the daylight of someone else's murdered birds. When you grow up in a big family sometimes there are shadows you never discuss.

When I look up the etymology of grief it tells me about the weight of things, it tells me to see "grave." When I look up the etymology of my father it tells me to see grief and smoked oysters, which he loved. Speaking of words:

I didn't think my father had anything to do with them. I didn't want to give that to him, these words of mine, this language that sometimes saves and strangles me. It's only in his death I remember his letters to me written on notecards or on yellow legal pads. Sometimes he wrote me silly poems that rhymed: *Roses are red, Violets are blue*, something something something, *I love you*. It's only in his death I realize my father was a writer. Once, the job he hated gave him an award and he wrote a speech, which I almost read last night but another sister said she needed it, so I'll probably never see it. One note he sent on an index card: "Though you are my fourth daughter chronologically, you will always be first in my heart. Love, Dad." See:

Like all great writers, my father knew how to lie, just like my sister. The truth is we, my brothers and sisters, were all first in his heart. He loved each one of us the first way he knew how, which wasn't always the best and was sometimes, to be honest, the absolute worst. Sometimes he loved us like displaced Lego parts or sweet Cherry Jolly Ranchers, and sometimes like birds contemplating suicide. Like my sister said, he was a hard man to live with. I loved him as much as I could, and sometimes I wished he would die. I'm just being honest. Maybe I only wanted him to go somewhere else for a spell. He could have done better. He did the first he could. That's what they say. Sometimes:

In a big family you breathe away skin and tissue and bone to get at each others' hearts, to scrape or swallow them whole like the heads of small suicidal birds. Sometimes *Nothing remembers. Everything remembers.* And sometimes, you breathe each other awake if you're lucky. Sometimes, more than once, we've been lucky. We have been. What I'm saying is I don't really believe in luck. That's not how this works. All I'm saying is my father did hit me, just once though, and what he might have said is probably most likely true—maybe it did hurt him more than it hurt me. I don't know how you measure something like that, but I know a Sparrow's heart might weigh .21 grams and a Mourning Dove's heart could weigh .50 grams, both of which are just as much as a human heart if we consider the overall weight of our bodies, not including the etymology of our grief. It's all relative. I'm pretty sure that's true. I just wanted to set the record straight. That's it. Thank you.

Funeral Mass: Man 2

He says he first met your father in 1960 as an Internal Revenue Agent. He says he immediately got to understand your father a lot because starting in the mid-60s they carpooled from South Bay to L.A. every day, he says, and he got to know what your father stood for, and, he says, I appreciated it and respected it from that day forward. Now, he says, backing up to his comment about certain things in life that he was naïve about: Born in Hawaii, I grew up in a sheltered community and everyone kind of looked like me and even talked like me, he says, so I was quite unaware of relationships we had in the mainland in the United States and before you knew it the Watts Uprising arose and I learned so much from your father. He says he wasn't familiar with the racial tension, which existed, because he never experienced it, but he got to learn a lot from your father, and, he says, it opened his eyes to a lot about human relationships.

Uncle Kwanza: November 1

This isn't a photograph but it might as well be the way it's framed
in my head: *The First Time We Journey to New Orleans.*

You let us empty pennies from glass jars as tall as our small bodies,
thousands from glass jars now rows of urns against the wall.

We, my sisters and I, sit and count one, two, three, four, all the way up
to fifty, stuffing faded paper rolls with your found treasure.

In the background of this photo that isn't, you laugh, call my father
Bubba, the brother he was before he escaped to L.A.

You were already Muslim, *first fruit of the harvest*, a name you claimed
your own self, shedding Milton to some faux paradise.

In the counting, we blame each other for making us lose our places, and I
wonder if you're rich, all these pennies, so much for my young hands.

I think only someone who gathers money he might never count must
know something about love, wanting, or end of days.

And I wanted to know things like why I sensed my father's fear returning
to the place that made him, or what words to ask about this ache.

No one knows how you made it from the Casino to Emergency, but
let's say you won big, let's say your pockets were filled with silver.

Let's not think about your blocked heart, broken, let's say you felt the
meaning of your name, new bounty, as free as any man, Black, can feel.

Tell Bubba hello, tell him I don't know what to do with the space he
used to take up, but say I'm figuring it out, tell him.

Remove the coins from your dead eyes, remove our eyes give them our dead, to remove our dead give them our only eyes, maybe, maybe . . .

Maybe I'll walk to the river, toss some pennies, maybe let's wish something first and full remove our dead eyes fruit for all of us.

Funeral Mass: Man 2

He says your father was always for the underdog and the less fortunate minorities, both in society and at work especially as Funeral Man 1 has mentioned. He says your father fought for the minorities, even to the extent of risking rebuke from his superiors. Your father was very adamant and strong in his convictions, he says, and he promoted a lot of minorities, and he encouraged, like Funeral Man 1 said, he says, a lot of minorities, but it got to be such a burden, he says, because you know when you're fighting your superiors sometimes you can get beaten down and I've experienced that myself in a management capacity to the point that I think your father decided it's better, he did his share, and he could retire earlier than he really wanted to. Your father arose, like Funeral Man 1 said, he says. Your father arose soon recognized to be a good leader and became a group manager and then a branch chief before he retired. Your father arose, he says. Your father arose.

On the Anniversaries of My Father's Death

I.

This sky.

The edge of Lake Michigan.

What do we do with memory?

I want a wild shawl to cover me

during this fog.

What's nearest isn't.

I look for a window,

See a coffin.

II.
This voice.

The edge of light.

What do we do with December?

I want a holy cloud to cover me

after this breath.

What's farthest isn't.

I look for a wall,

See a lake.

III.
This joy.

The edge of wind.

What do we do with stillness?

I want burnt linens to cover me

among these ruins.

What's latest isn't.

I look for an attic,

see a photograph.

Letter to L.: Unsent

I wanna tell you I get it, what you told me that summer and every season after, the quickening October dark, falling leaves inside your bones. How some days you can't leave the house, other days you can't stop crying, the ways you attack hair and skin when your body goes numb. Your *Dark Days*—the months before and after your father's death—that's what you call them.

I'm just warning you. If we're going to be friends, you should know this about me, what happens.

That summer, kids took buses from projects, Bayview Hunter's Point Portrero Hill Sunnydale, high-sounding places anywhere else might be beautiful. They came for poetry. Words, we said. Language. Sometimes we sounded certain, told them what they already knew, how sound can hold maybe save us sometimes, but rarely buys us bread or love. We sent them home to the definite promise of bullets.

That summer you cried a lot, played your father's records, Jazz and Blues, made me salads, dried cranberry hearts on mounds of dark green. We laughed and danced in sun in concert, the Fugees at Golden Gate Park. *Ready or Not?* Sometimes I pick that summer as the beginning of the end of belief. It's easy to blame you who refused to hide, always hanging your skin like the laundry on the fire escape outside your bedroom window inside out to dry.

You didn't want anything more from me than what I could give, a hand on your shoulder while you breathed panic in and out, to listen to you cry, say it isn't your fault, hold you, or do nothing. What could I say or do I wouldn't say or do again next year and the year after that, but that didn't matter did it? You just wanted me there. For me, that was everything.

I did okay.

That's a lie. I was never there, even when I was, not just with you. I couldn't break the self you'd already cracked wide open. I listened to you cry and wished you could be like the rest of us: take some pills, drink, smoke, go about your day, battle blood-mares in the dark. I wanted to be like you. I didn't want to be anything like you. I did what I could, afraid we'd swallow each other whole like Sula and Nel—your father dead, my father living but long absent. One of us had to be strong. That's a lie too.

You didn't want anything more from me than what I want now, someone who will let me disappear, be in the room sometimes a covered ball of light in a corner, maybe say something maybe not, hold my head in her lap, run fingernails down my back like the grandmother I barely knew used to, press a hand to my forehead, say breathe.

In your last note, after I wrote you my father died, in your one and only sentence you said you were sorry for my loss and wished me peace, like one of those white-gloved slaps in plantation movies, like I held my hand to my mouth and said Damn, it's like that then. Like we were strangers. We hadn't talked for a year. The fight we had before this doesn't matter, something stupid and important. We were both right and wrong. We were done. If death doesn't bring return then nothing can. I was glad for the break; months of quiet slips into years. When a friendship that long ends that easy I wonder, but it hasn't been easy.

Some nights I can't sleep. Some mornings I can't remember why anyone should open her eyes. This morning sky thick with rain. I wait at my desk for something to happen—sleet then flurries then snow. I want to call you and tell you it's snowing in spring, this weather sucks, some days I hate living here so much I wanna start walking anywhere, and other days I run free on trails of ice, splintering, reminds me of life below. Days like this I can't remember sun or sky.

Sometimes it Snows in April.

I wanna call you and sing the Prince song, discuss the proportions of his tiny frame, imagine his tongue together, stay on the phone for hours like we used to. Those days are gone. It's only April and already I'm somewhere else counting the months to my sister's phone call, how they found our father choking on his own breath and then nothing, the message I can't erase after almost two years, an arm a leg the space behind my eyes I can feel it my body creasing, the changing inward December fold. So this is how it goes.

I get it now. I do.

IV. Sinew

I am black alive and looking back at you.

—June Jordan

To the Killers of Us

for D.

What did you do to us?
Did you drink our skin,
make tea from the powdered layers?

Did you weave our coffins
with hair from our own heads,
was this you?

And what of the whorls
that used to grace our fingers?
What happened to the trace of us?

Are we the ones who scream at your deathbed?
Were we the ones who said we forgive you,
who sometimes beat and call our women bitches,
tell them to fuck off and get the fuck out, who remove
our tongues to kiss men in dented corners, wake
with your name stuck in our teeth or branded on our cheek,
who tell stories of bright rooms and closed familiar hands when
we're too young, or gaping sidewalks when we're old enough
to watch you choke us again and again while we yell,
We can't—, or say nothing,
was this us?

Who were we then?
What are we becoming?

Some days we wonder what is left for us to love.
Some days we wonder what's left of us.

Tell us.

You who have taken almost everything,
but this white butterfly holding onto purple
for dear life, or the sweat that comes from
bucking bales, or seeding sweet corn we planted
with hands we trace from singing
the million ways Black and Brown hearts die
and live, still we live
stories no one believes or wants to hear,
like the love that rinses our tilted tear gassed faces
into a milky caul,
or the small passing of sage our nephew bound,
juniper, yellow and red roses,
into our open hands,
true true medicine, ours to burn
and bathe in smoke,
stoke each heart and limb
for that next time fire.
See—

You have not taken any of these things,
not the music or the beat or the drum we hollowed
from cottonwood, cut on our land, strung with animals
we soaked and dried our own selves, these skins,
the remains of our staggered breath,
yes,
we, the *survivor of many,*
who will love and live still,
we know what you've done,
we're telling who you are.

Taos, New Mexico

Dispatch: New Orleans

from an introduction I gave at the Creative Writing Awards Ceremony in New Orleans at the College Language Association Conference, which was "founded in 1937 by a group of Black scholars and educators" in response to the exclusionary, racist practices of the Modern Language Association.

We're in the city where my parents were born and raised. My father, who passed a few years ago, was raised uptown, and my mother was raised in the Seventh Ward, in St. Bernard Projects, which no longer exist because they were torn down after Katrina. I used to think I didn't have very many stories, but being at this conference, and being in this city where every time I return I feel as if I'm walking through a portal, I'm reminded once again, we're always in a place with stories. This afternoon, at the panel "Blues and Jazz in African American Poetry," Eugene B. Redmond presented questions he poses to younger poets: "Are you connected to the tradition?" and "Are you happy?" *Are you connected to the tradition? Are you happy?*

+

Strangled: Letter to a Young Black Poet

for D. A.

A zombie is a technological soldier
ingrained in race
trying the spirits of beautiful folks like you.
A zombie moves in the same moment wrong
together with other zombies insane,
the apex of not feeling.
This is all to say: you are not a zombie.
Wash, rinse, repeat.
You are not a zombie.
What you feel is valid.
Speak this trying country.
Slap the shit out of privileged spaces.
Study the hiatus of hermits.
Meet the words of loving others.
Work through talking rage.
Weep blocks of wood.
Live.
This is all to say blackpoets love you.
blackpoestspeakout to and for you.
This is all to say I myself love you.
Wash, rinse, repeat.
I love myself loving you.
Soon.
Breathe.

Breathe.

Breathe.

An Open Letter of Love to Black Students: #BlackLivesMatter

I wrote this letter, a version of which was signed by over 1000 Black professors around the world in December 2014, about a week after a grand jury decided not to pursue charges against Daniel Pantaleo, the White officer who murdered Eric Garner. This grand jury's announcement occurred less than a week or so after another grand jury declined to indict Darren Wilson, the White officer who murdered Michael Brown. Almost a year after these grand jury decisions, a wave of resistance on college campuses began with University of Missouri. New names were added and continue to be added.

We are Black professors.

We are daughters, sons, brothers, sisters, cousins, nieces, nephews, godchildren, grandfathers, grandmothers, fathers, and mothers, and all the greats.

We're writing to tell you we see you and hear you.

We know the stories of dolls hanging by nooses, nigger written on dry erase boards and walls, stories of nigger said casually at parties by White students too drunk to know their own names but who know their place well enough to know nothing will happen if they call you out your name; stories of nigger said stone sober, stories of them calling you nigger using every other word except what they really mean to call you, stories of you having to explain your experience in classrooms—your language, your dress, your hair, your music, your skin—yourself, of you having to fight for all of us in classrooms where you are often the only one or one of a few, stories of you choosing silence as a matter of survival.

Sometimes we're in those classrooms with you.

We know there is always more that people don't see or hear or want to know, but we see you. We hear you.

In our mostly White classrooms we work with some of you, you who tell us other professors don't see, don't hear you. You, who come to our offices with stories of erasure that make you break down. They don't see me, you say. They don't hear me. We know and don't know how to hold your tears.

How do we hold your tears, and your anger?

You are our sons and daughters, our brothers and sisters, our mothers, our fathers, our godchildren. You, with your stories of erasure break our hearts because you are family, because your stories of erasure ultimately are stories of violence, because your stories mirror our experiences, past and present.

Right now. This is all happening now. Every day. We know this.

We want you to hear.

You tell us your stories and sometimes we tell you our own stories of cops who stop us on the way to work, of grandparents born in Jim Crow, of parents born during segregation into an economic reality that made them encourage us to get solid jobs, of parents born outside the United States who came face to face with the harsh reality of U.S. anti-Blackness, how we chose institutions where we often feel alone. We tell you stories of almost dropping out of school, stories of working harder than anyone else even when it felt like it was killing us, even when it is killing us. We tell you we know historically and predominantly White universities might let you/ us in, but they don't care much about retaining us no matter how many times they misuse pretty words like diversity, or insult us with the hard slap of minority.

We tell you about the underground network of folks who helped us, the people who wrote us letters, the offices we cried in, the times we were silent, the times we spoke up, the times we thought we wouldn't make it, the people who told us to hold on. We tell you over and over about the railroad of Black professors and other professors of color who we call when we know one of us is in need. We remind you skinfolk isn't always kinfolk. We tell you to be careful. We tell you to take risks. We tell you, guard your heart. We tell you, keep your heart open. We tell you to hold on. Hold on, we say, to you, to us, because holding on to each other is everything, often the only thing.

Hold on.

We want a future for you, for us right now.

We write this is in solidarity with the families of Tamir Rice, Mike Brown, Renisha McBride, Trayvon Martin, Rekia Boyd, Aiyana Stanley Jones, and so many others who they are killing, so many others who should have had the chance to be in our classrooms, who should have had the chance to simply be.

We write this in solidarity with Harriet Tubman, Ida B. Wells, Frederick Douglass, Sojourner Truth, Malcolm X, Martin Luther King, and too many others stolen and gone, too many others who fought for us to be in this privileged place where we still have to fight for justice.

We write this in solidarity with The Combahee River Collective and #BlackLives-Matter, brilliant Black womxn, who knew and know we have to fight for and love all of us if any one of us is going to survive.

We write this in solidarity with you, Black students, here and elsewhere, and with those on the ground for over 100 days, four and a half hours, two seconds.

The living and the dead. We hear you. We see you.

You don't need us to tell you this but please, please keep refusing any tired, fake, post-race messages of moderation. We heard this during the Civil Rights movement whose promises we never fulfilled. We heard this during slavery whose structural echoes we still hear in our hollow institutions. We've been here before. We *been* here. We are here. We won't stay here. Keep resisting. Don't stop.

In our classes we'll continue to do what we've always done: teach about race, racism, anti-Blackness, and White Supremacy. This has and will continue to put us in positions we have to defend. This has and will continue to compromise our jobs, our health, our relationships with other people who profess to be our colleagues. This has and will compromise relationships with partners who tell us with love we need to set better boundaries.

We're trying.

We study ourselves. We study, we live Black lives. We organize. We strategize. We march. We teach to nurture and resist. We don't always talk about the letters we write to administrators, the angry emails we send, the committees and task forces we serve on, the department meetings where we question and push for more, the colleagues who question our research, our presence, our skin, our manner of being. We don't always talk about the weight of pushing for more, more being basic equity, more being the right to exist without explanation or apology, more being the right to love and be loved.

What we do is not enough. It's never enough, but we'll keep on. We'll keep finding ways to do more. For all of us.

We're supposed to say views expressed herein are ours alone, but we believe that truth to be self-evident.

Some people who share our views will not sign this but they're still with us. The living and the dead.

We've never been alone.

You already know your life matters. Know we're fighting with you and for you. With all of us. For all of us.

We got you.

We see you. We hear you. We love you.

⸸

Dispatch: Minneapolis

an excerpt from a speech I recorded for the Black Graduate Student Association.

It's Tuesday.

I'm in Minneapolis, Minnesota for a writer's conference. The last time I was in Minnesota I'd just finished my very White MFA program. I'd been awarded a writing residency at Norcroft, which sat on the shore of Lake Superior in Lutsen, Minnesota. Joan Drury, a White lesbian writer and philanthropist, founded Norcroft to create a needed space for women to write. One thing I appreciated about Norcroft, especially as a writer who was just beginning to write, was it didn't matter if you'd published or not. Drury recognized the many barriers in place for women to get to that point. Norcroft offered women time and space.

Each bedroom at Norcroft was named after a woman writer: Amy Tan, Audre Lorde, Barbara Kingsolver, and Julia Alvarez. I had the Audre Lorde room. Our writing sheds, which were really beautiful little studios, sat away from the main house near the water or in the woods. My shed was in the woods. I'd walk there with a thermos full of coffee or tea and spend the morning or night writing. A key component of this residency was silence. We couldn't speak to the other women until 4:00 each afternoon, so most of the day we spent in necessary silence that allowed me to write and go inward in ways I hadn't been able to do, in ways I've only realized recently would prepare me for future work. After two years of my very White MFA program, I was thankful for the silence.

I can still see the small bookshelf near the front door of the main house at Norcroft. This is where I stumbled upon Houston Baker's *Workings of the Spirit: Poetics of Afro-American Women's Writing*, which gave me language for writing I was just falling into. At the time, I was also reading about Harriet Tubman and thought I'd write some fiction in which she appeared. These feel like extra details but I'm thinking about place and space, silence and protection and spirit right now on this particular mournful Tuesday, where video of lying White cop Michael Slager shooting Walter Lamar Scott, father of four, in the back, eight times, is everywhere I look.

To get to this writing residency, I flew into and out of Duluth, Minnesota. I'd never heard of Duluth, Minnesota. Who and what is Duluth, Minnesota? I'm sure

Duluth is, does, and has many things, but one thing it definitely owns is the 1920 lynching of Elias Clayton, Elmer Jackson, and Isaac McGhie. I learned about their murders in a book I bought at Drury Lane Books, a feminist bookstore owned by Joan Drury, in Grand Marais, while I was at Norcroft. When the residency finished and I had to spend another night in Duluth before I flew out the next morning, I walked around town with slightly different eyes, up to where White townsmen dragged, beat, and hung three young Black men who came to Duluth as part of a travelling circus and found themselves at the end of a rape accusation.

We know the truth. We knew the story of Walter Scott's murder before it was told to us. It's only the details that change.

In Duluth, the lynching corner is just a corner. I stood near an empty lot, where a memorial would be built later that fall, a memorial I hope to one day see, and I thought about place and history, story and fictions. I thought about traces traumatic events might leave in a place. I thought about historical trauma and personal trauma and the blurry line between, and the ways many of us, myself included, construct our lives around silences and the weight of this silence on our bodies, on our communities. Mostly, I thought about the boys whose lives they stole: Elias, Elmer, and Isaac. I thought about their families, how long it took for them to find out their sons and brothers were dead. I thought about future lives lost. *How* do you go on? How *do* we go on? I felt silly for standing in a place I wasn't even sure was the right spot. I felt silly for wanting to feel something more than the nothing I felt, which I've come to understand isn't nothing but more like the "circles and circles of sorrow" Nel feels at the end of *Sula*, like the circles and circles of sorrow I feel on this particular day of mourning, which is just another Tuesday in this country.

After I went to the lynching corner, I walked down the main street, and in a store window I saw a poster for an event commemorating the lynching. It just so happened the day I was in Duluth was the anniversary of the lynching and Duluth was holding a read-in of the book I'd bought when I was at the residency. I went inside the store and asked the White woman behind the counter if I could have the poster. She'd been talking to another White woman. There was that uncomfortable pause that occurs with White folks when a person of color makes race visible. I smiled. She didn't ask my reason for wanting it. She said okay. I don't know what I would've done or said if she'd said no. I said thank you. I kept smiling and turned my back to the women in order to peel the poster from the window.

Many of us don't know the stories of murdered cis and trans Black women and girls as well as we should: Rekia Boyd, Renisha McBride, Shereese Francis, Megan Hockaday, Aiyana Jones, Aura Rosser, Tanisha Anderson, Islan Nettles, Ty Underwood, Lamia Beard, Goddess Edwards, Sandra Bland, and counting. I can't keep up with names of our dead.

Before I went to the read-in I had a beer at a bar next door to the theatre. I talked to a young White guy from Duluth. We talked about writing. I told him about the writing residency for women. I think we talked about Tolkien and *Lord of the Rings* and Edgar Allen Poe. White male writers. I might have mentioned Toni Morrison. I didn't want to talk about race with him. I didn't want to talk about the reading of the lynching happening right next door. I didn't want to know if he knew any stories. I didn't want to know if I was talking to someone whose great great grandfather was one of the descendants of the grinning staring White people in the famous postcard where Elmer's and Elias's broken bodies hang from a light pole and where Isaac's body lies face down on the ground because his body was hung so high he wouldn't fit in the photo otherwise. I finished my beer, happy to be a little numb, and went to the read-in and listened to a loving community from Duluth read the story of the lynching out loud.

At this conference where I am, I'll be talking about race and creative writing pedagogy and practice with three other Black women. This is work I care deeply about, but I don't care much about this particular conference, which some people refer to as the All White People conference. This conference, which costs a sick amount of money to attend, is not why I write. I'm here for the community, for people I've met online who I'm looking forward to knowing in person, to writers I know but haven't seen for too long. Community is why I'm here, and also why it kills me I can't be where you are because you and your work, us, matters most to me.

So when I get an email that says "people like you help us to understand that we are not alone in this journey," it makes me pause and consider what it is I've actually done, which isn't enough. It makes me wonder again what I'm doing at this conference, where I'm putting my energy, and it makes me commit to doing more, to continue thinking about place and space, silence and protection, and spirit work. *The work protects.*

I'm trying to believe this. I'm continuing to think about Black Spaces we inherit, create, and transform together, spaces that offer protection, that might serve as both sword and shield, in and outside of these institutions, on any particular Tuesday.

Clayton Jackson McGhie

Memorial Week of Events 2003

Saturday June 7, 7:00 p.m.
African-American Film Screening, "Strange Fruit.", Suggested donation $6. At NorShor Theatre,
211 East Superior Street.

Sunday June 8, 7:00 p.m.
Hope and Remembrance Concert, First Lutheran Church, 1100 East Superior Street. Gospel Soul and Jazz
fundraising event. Cost $10.

Tuesday June 10, 7:00 p.m.
"The Word of Truth " - poetry reading at Beaner's Central, 324 North Central Avenue. Free to the public.

Wednesday June 11, 7:00 p.m.
"We Have a Story to Tell" - Duluth's African-American men tell their stories. Washington Center,
310 North First Avenue West.

Friday June 13, noon
Clayton Jackson McGhie Memorial March. Gather in front of Duluth's old City Jail across from the
casino entrance.

Saturday June 14, 5:00 - 10:00 p.m.
Illustrated marathon reading of Michael Fedo's "The Lynchings in Duluth". Includes projected display of
contemporary photographs and period costuming. At the NorShor Theatre, 211 East Superior Street.
Suggested donation $10.

Thank you to all of our Sponsors!
Duluth Superior Area Community Foundation, Otto Bremer Foundation,
Ordean Foundation, CJM Memorial, SMDC, Community Action Duluth, Duluth News Tribune,
City of Duluth, Duluth Budgeteer News and Community-spirited Individuals

Dispatch: Dearborn Heights

We were just here in September. We were here this past summer. We were here in some February not too long ago. We were here in 2010. We've been here so many times. We're tired and sad and angry. The truth we know: We are never not here in this place where people devalue and criminalize Black bodies and lives. If we do a roll call of the dead, how many names?

our liberation is a necessity not an adjunct to somebody else's

We know the script. People are already arguing about details: her precious body dumped from somewhere else, her precious body found on the porch, shot in the back of the head, shot in the face, reason for the car accident, time in between the car accident and her arrival on the murderer's front porch, shooting the gun an act of self-defense, an accident.

One fact: Renisha McBride, a nineteen-year-old, unarmed Black woman, someone's daughter, someone's niece, someone's friend, is dead.

Quiet as it's kept: her casket had to be closed at her funeral.

What we know: Stand your ground=Black death.

What we don't know: ~~the name of her murderer.~~ Theodore Wafer.

Who is Killing Us?

Who do we create sacred spaces for? Who gets to know what justice feels like? Who gets to be remembered? Who do we love?

Renisha McBride.

Last night dream hampton asked us to remember why we were here, gathered in front of the Dearborn Heights Police Station, asked us to raise our voices and speak Renisha McBride's name. Remember why we're here, she said. Our humanity is at stake.

to be recognized as levelly human is enough to be recognized as levelly human is enough

We're not waiting for recognition. We know the truth. We've always known it. We learned it from people who loved us enough to arm us for this world, people who taught us the difference between paranoia and protection. We're not paranoid. Let's say it again: We are not paranoid. We are prepared. We are at war.

Shaming is one of the deepest tools of imperialist White capitalist patriarchy.

The assault on our bodies, minds, and hearts has always been. We learned the truth from our mothers, all our mothers, who showed us even under assault we are never not here.

Flesh.

Flesh that needs to be loved.

Bones. Skin. Sinew.

Say her name:

Renisha McBride.

Renisha McBride.

Renisha McBride.

On Being a Vine

for my niece, who got the part of a vine in The Secret Garden,
performed at her predominantly White elementary school

Your worried face wonders if you can do this. How does a vine think? What does it feel?
Do vines own hearts, and if so do they beat fast or slow? What about souls? Maybe when
we wake in the night and want a glass of water or our mothers or fathers or our younger
brothers maybe when we wake our breath caught between this world and some other
maybe it's the vine souls choking us to remember their life. And do they dream of sun or
sky or clouds all of it up and away reaching toward light or maybe roots and earth wet
and dark and deep? Are their nightmares of us? And what if the frozen-faced crowd
makes you forget the vine dance your small arms trying to wrap around giant air on a
glaring stage? What then? What if you stand still, let the world race around you, you,
your own secret light in the eye tangled prayer of hands beneath your chin? Listen: What
we know of vines ain't got nothin on you sweetest brown girl greenest thing this world
will ever see.

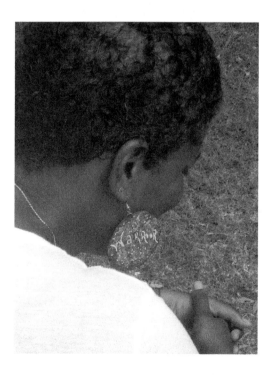

Swing Low Suite

For Harriet Tubman, the Combahee River Collective, and for the twen-
ty Black women who I gathered with on Port Royal Island in June 2013,
answering a call from Alexis Pauline Gumbs and Julia Sangodare Wallace
to join them in commemorating the "150th anniversary of Harriet Tubman's
successful uprising where 750 enslaved Africans freed themselves and each
other at the Combahee River." And for A: one of the twenty-one of us, fairy-
winged one, who in 2017 took her life into her own hands. www.mobilehom-
ecoming.org/upcoming-events/combahee-pilgrimage-13/

Welcome loved ones

1

In the Lowcountry
Women wear white
Cut their souls on rock
Annointed in Blood
Mud and Salt
River and Tears

What is something you wanna get free from as part of this journey?

2

I know rivers and tears
My feet in the Combahee
White skirt lifted to my waist
Dark water shadows around my thighs

*we were told be quiet for the sake of being "ladylike"/be quiet to be less objection-
able in the eyes of white people*

3

In the lowcountry
Women stand circle strong
Lift every voice and sing
See us in our eyes
Hear us our song

And what is the community that you would risk everything for even your own transformation?

4

What side are you on my sister
What side are you on
What side are you on my brother
What side are you on

if Black women were free, if Black women were free, if Black women were free

5

In the Lowcountry
We sing freedomside
Sing down love down rain
Sing down *the underground rail*
Take me to the water to Harriet Sweet Harriet
Sing and swing these stones
Call this one Fear this one Pain
Shame and Doubt
Lay them low *how low can you go*
All the way down down by the riverside

we have memories within that came out of the material that went to make us

6

I know rivers and bridges
On a bridge in Jamaica
Down below the Rio Grande

All the women in white
My aunt who has seen everything
Holds up her hand says Wait
I want to remember this
Bright white cotton headwraps
Black skin banana leaf Green
Mountain Brown Blue Caribbean Sky
Me watching me watch my aunt watch them
Bridge a soft place for all of us
Now I close my eyes, my breath, dunk my head,
I rise remembering
All water has perfect memory
I rise
Study our steady selves

it would mean that everyone else would have to be free

7

Be the woman in the water
The woman standing on the bank
She/he/they laughing on the dock
Her/him/them holding them in trees
Be the fairy-winged one
Flitting from rock to rock
Be the woman kissing the other woman
The woman floating naked on her back
Be the landing of her breasts
Be her pulled by the current
Be the one holding her hand
Be her hand beating the drum
Be the drum skin taut and ready
Be the drum
Beat

*Harriet Tubman was a freedom fighter/She taught us how to fight/oh yeah/We
gonna fight all day and night until we get it right/oh yeah*

8

We the righteous bridge
We the water under the bridge
We the story before the bridge
We the enslaved running
Whatever we can take
Steaming pots of rice
Woven baskets
Chickens under each arm
Lucky sets of twins around our mothers' necks
Pairs like we never see
A young one hangin' on behind
One han' roun' her forehead to hold on
'tother han diggin into the rice-pot
Eatin' with all its might
Hold of her dress two or three more
Down her back a bag with a pig in it
We the blood-storm
Thunder lightning
Every drop of rain
We the hands gripping the boats
Don't you leave us here
We the deep tenor seagrass tending us all
Onto the ships
We the one in command
Tellin us we're free

the only people who care enough about us to work consistently for our liberation are us

9

In the Lowcountry
Rivers of women
Carry us back to us
Each one every one
Sing us dance us
All the way home
To be baptized

Dispatch: East Lansing

A week ago today, I was in the hospital having surgery for thyroid cancer. It had taken a long time to get to this point where the anesthesiologist was suddenly saying, "So I'm going to put the oxygen mask on you now."

Today is my father's birthday. I had the surgery three days after the two-year anniversary of his death. This is one way I measure time now.

I thought I'd have to wait until this past Monday to hear the results of the pathology report, the results that would tell me whether or not I did in fact have cancer, and whether or not I'd have to undergo radiation to kill any remaining cancerous cells. The doctor called me last Friday and let me know what they found was indeed cancerous, but they caught it in time and it was small enough, so no radiation.

I thought I'd write something longer about all of this, but each time I try I only get to one or two possible sentences:

The first doctor tells me my neck is enlarged.

When the doctor inserts the needle for the biopsy. . .

And then nothing, and I get tired just thinking about the journey that led to the first incision. Clearly, it's still too soon.

Today, my great aunt on the Jamaican side of the family enlisted a small group of family and friends to conduct a thinking Reiki for me and my husband. Auntie Glo is in her nineties and still teaches yoga. I don't know how anyone's supposed to say no to Auntie Glo. In an email she explains a thinking Reiki means "we each focus our thoughts on the receiver. The meditation helps each of us to keep our thinking focused. Each of us writes in our own way and so we might make the meditation practice around the process of creating a piece of writing—a poem, a blessing, a bouquet of healing thoughts."

So from 3:00 to 3:30, family and friends sent healing energy from Jamaica, Canada, D.C., California. Such a simple loving gift: Today, we're all going to think about you, we're going to remember you, at the same time. If people were sending me healing thoughts, the least I could do was try to be open.

I thought about the past couple of years. I thought about what it means to grieve—a person, or a piece of one's own body, how it feels similar. I thought about hospitals and doctors and needles and fear.

I release each pound of fury. I release each dying cell. I release each memory of death, each death of memory. I release, I release, I release.

If only it was this easy, but it's a start.

In the past couple of years, I've learned more about the thyroid than I care to know. I never knew how important it is, and I had no idea how prevalent thyroid cancer is among women. I had no idea Black women might be less likely to get thyroid cancer, but we're more likely to die from it.

We are learning by heart/what has never been taught.

Around 4:00 a.m. on Sunday, five days after the surgery, eight days after the two-year anniversary of my father's death, the power went out in our house, the result of an ice storm that hit mid-Michigan. I've never been in an ice storm. It's devastating. The trees encased in ice become weighted down. The other day a friend told me an inch of ice on a live wire or tree branch adds so much weight, hundreds of pounds.

We stayed in our house the first couple of days without power, our conversations interrupted by the breaking of branches of old trees in our front and back yard. It's hard to describe this sound. The same friend who told me about the weight of ice described it as a "pop and a hiss." It's devastating. Pieces of trees that have spent so many years forming gone in an instant.

It's also beautiful. When I see all of these plants encased in ice it almost makes me believe we can preserve things. Maybe come spring everything will be okay. It almost makes me completely believe my neighbor when in response to my lamenting the breaking branches he says, "Oh, they'll regenerate." Because that's what's supposed to happen, old bark grows over new wounds, and life goes on. Of course that's not how it works exactly all the time. Plants and people die. But yes, life still goes on, changed but continuing, and we're changed in the wake of the death, changed and continuing. People live on in various ways inside us. Skin and cells. Memories passed from one generation to the next. Blood and breath. If we're lucky, we might even have their words, like the index cards my father used to mail me with rhyming poems and short notes I thought were so silly then, but which I still kept, and which now hang above my writing desk at home.

Even now in Michigan, many remain without power. We had to leave our house because it was thirty-two degrees inside, too cold for me to recover in the way I need. I'm thankful we have the means to be in a hotel room. It's not the Christmas I thought we'd have, but I'm here, we're here together. It's more than enough.

V. Souls

You just can't fly on off and leave a body.

—Toni Morrison

Divided Heart: Part II

Or maybe it doesn't connect. The way disconnection not only tells the story but is the story.

I'm on a plane to L.A. Heading to a conference for writers I could never imagine existing when I was growing up here. Where are you from, people ask? L.A., I say to make it easy. But L.A.'s so huge—what part, they ask? Carson? I say, always in the form of a question. And then I name cities nearby: Compton, Inglewood, Long Beach. Places a little more visible, more on the map for some.

For months I've been thinking about the title to the panel I'll be on: "Remapping Displacement: Women Writers from L.A. Redefine 'Home.'" I've been thinking about the settler colonial project of mapping, how a certain kind of mapping has always been in the interest of empire. To name and claim and survey and chart a place as one's own as if the land and people living with and on and for the land have never existed and aren't already equipped with their own methods of mapping.

What it means to map a place or a person. What it means to map trauma. What it means to re-map displacement, which you are always in the process of mapping because you can never quite place it. *When did it happen? Yesterday, but it feels like today.*

I can only map displacement in disconnection, in the silences of my family's personal stories and my own, and in the silences in historical narratives. In the fragmented sentence, the enjambed line. The spaces between.

Again, I'm remembering stories as mirrors and maps, as Leslie Marmon Silko describes them, both reflecting and guiding, reminding us of spaces that no longer exist, marking spots still present, and also thinking of them in the way Octavia Butler might consider them—shaping places that haven't yet come to be or already exist in ways we might not recognize.

Carson Mall, where I used to hang out and work, long ago became the more gentrified sounding "South Bay Pavillion," complete with major chain stores. Cal State Dominguez Hills, which was moved to Carson from Palos Verdes after the Watts Rebellion, and is just up the street from my house, sits on Chumash and Gabrielino-Tongva lands, which became Rancho San Pedro, an early California so-called land grant, all history I'm just beginning to immerse myself in.

Mapping is an intimate endeavor. To trace the outline of someone's lips, the small of someone's back. I could draw her face from memory, we say. I know these streets like the back of my own hand. As soon as I step foot, it will feel like I never left. And to erase someone from a map involves a violent intimacy I've long been considering.

Another kind of mapping has always been about resistance and freedom. North Star and safe-houses. Coded language. Signifying. Mapping that sustains self and community. The stories we tell and retell, the stories by Black, Indigenous, and other people of color I turn to and return to when I feel as if I've lost my way. We've been here before, these stories tell me. You'll make it out of this place alive and whole, maybe, and if you don't there'll be others after you charged with remembering.

My mother has started to tell me more stories. A couple of days ago she forwarded an email whose subject heading is "Picture." In the email she says her cousin died and her cousin's daughter sent her a picture. It's an old black and white photo of eleven children, all Black of various hues, dressed up for a holiday maybe, all standing in front of a house in New Orleans in the 7th Ward sometime in the mid-1940s. My mother was born in 1939. Rather than identify herself in the photo, my mother writes: "Do you recognize me?"

It's been two years since I've been to L.A. It's the beginning of April and it's snowing in Michigan. After living in the Midwest for almost five years, I feel the protective hunkering down that comes with winter even in the L.A. brightness. But it doesn't take long to remember the feel of L.A.: sun, blue sky, the nearness of the ocean, traffic, waiting in traffic, always that sense of waiting, always that sense of knowing or hoping more exists beneath the shiny surface of things.

L.A. as place, as idea, is forever distant and close, solid and ephemeral, but still when people ask, "So where are you from?" it's the first place I name, the first place where, if I had to, I could close my eyes and know I could find my way home.

The Tree of Return

"King Agadja of Dahomey planted the Tree of Return in the grand Place de Zoungbodji, marking the point of last goodbyes. By turning three times around the tree, slaves could ensure that their spirits would return to their homeland after death."

—"Visiting Ouidah," The Ouidah Museum of History,
www.museeouiday.org/Visiting Ouidah.htm

Like when you close your eyes and see yourself on stage with the Jackson 5 *stop the love you save may be your own* like when you think a song is written just for you *ooo la la la* like this is my jam and no one else better claim it cause you said it first and that's the way it works down here *Rock Rock Planet Rock* on someone's boom box some summer everyone outside in the street on the curb underneath the streetlamp and you're supposed to go inside when it comes on but you don't always you want to linger after sweat and lips and hide-and-go-get-it but that comes later

When are we?

1980 something redlined L.A. suburb meaning all Black see everyone's parents from somewhere-else-Louisiana-Mississippi-Alabama see Buddy on the manhole cover we call home plate waiting for Phil who years later will be shot who years later a cop will kill for standing in the wrong place for standing wrong at the wrong time which is always what matters is now Phil standing alive and Buddy waiting for Phil to throw a good fastball which is just a tennis ball and Buddy can't hit so the pitch is irrelevant what matters is you sitting on the fire hydrant near Mrs. Franklin's mailbox which is also third base and Erica standing next to you saying hey batter batter batter hey batter batter pink and blue beads at the end of her braids click-clacking like this moment could be a numbered panel in the Migration of the Negro but you don't know anything about that Lawrence Negro yet what matters is the cop car at the end of the street what matters is Erica saying here comes the fuzz and you laugh with her then take your cue from the older boys who move their bored bodies as slow as they want unzip the street just enough for the fuzz to pass windows rolled down watching you watch them watch you like someone pressed pause except no one turns the song down *don't stop* the cops round the corner and you all go back to before they showed up with their sorry slunk-down selves Buddy says man throw me something I can hit and Erica with her hey batter batter because not one of you is fully grown but all of you have already learned the suspect magic of transforming threats to Black life into nothing but a minor interruption

like my father with his lead diabetes foot stomping *Iko Iko* carnival rhythms *my grandma and your grandma* my father's mother my first time in New Orleans she laid sick up in her bed said come here baby closer so I can see your pretty face these all your babies to my mother like the box of Mardi Gras beads she sent every year my sisters and I laid them on the floor like jewels like the gold pinky ring the boy next door found in the street and gave me then his family moved back down South but not before he kissed me now every time I hear Luther and Gregory I'm twelve years old because *there's nothing better than love* when he left I was certain the South had everything beautiful Black and secret on lock forget water hoses that was TV and a long time ago Birmingham couldn't be all bad if it created him besides I'd already been to New Orleans and heard the music and ate boiled shrimp so I knew my parents were lying about the South being a place no one in her right mind would ever want to live even before my grandmother died and I found my father crying by himself looking out the window at the street I used to play on but it looked nothing like the street with the stoops in his city hundreds of miles away where his mother would be buried in a grave like a small house above ground so no water would wash her away not his tears or the cheap wine he drank every night to help him forget I don't know maybe the scars on his back where his father the son of a White father and Black mother whose name no one knows beat him I knew the South was a real place you could leave but also a feeling stuck inside your skin like if someone asks where y'at you might say South and the meaning will vary depending on the context like my mother off key singing *truly truly in love with you girl* like I'm covering my ears and rolling my eyes at my sisters like when is she going to stop and my mother truly not giving a fuck at all like what would my mother's life resemble in a context absent of segregation and fear of Black bodies

Who are we?

slow jams mix tapes recording songs off the oldies station Jackie Wilson Belafonte
Nat King Cole Lena Horne brown faces on your parents' records it's no accident
you wrote your first poem listening to Stevie Wonder or later you fell in love with
a piano player otherwise known as The Relationship That Made Me Swear Off All
Future Musicians because who wants to be second to anyone's first love but Music
Man gave you Thelonius Monk so this might be about give and take and then there
was the poet who knew what to do with a conga and shared his reggae dreams and
by then *bend down low* it was too late like his Jamaican grandmother who loved to
dance used to say when she was still alive love was born

Let me tell you what I know

I might not believe in God but I believe in the blue note Strange Fruit hip hop
Purple Rain and the dub side.

I believe in *I'll Fly Away* sung by a Creole man at my father's open casket wake. I
believe in the side dip and bounce when you're dancing a second line. I believe in
Louis Armstrong playing for Lucille in front of the Sphinx.

I believe in Miles not with his back to us but facing the soul-crushing thing for us
even as he failed us, again and again.

I believe in the love Whitney was saving, Marvin Gaye's healing, Gil Scot's revolu-
tion, and I'm almost certain some salvation might be at the end of Mariah Carey's
high note circa 1988.

I believe in *me myself and I* and *don't forget what you got.*

I believe in Aretha spelling our name, and in Nina because *Mississippi goddam* here
come four women carrying the sun until we make a joyful weep.

I believe in Billie always Billie let's all bow our heads to Billie who we failed—

Finally, I swear by the hearts of first generation Southern migration Black girls
who after Saturday morning cartoons wait outside their house for another girl and
when she sees her says watch me and does the splits or a back bend or some move

she makes up on the spot and the other girl does three cartwheels and then they wait for one more girl to open her front door and this holiest trinity turns cheap plastic jump ropes into a Harriett Tubman double-dutch dance of freedom like beats in Congo Square thick-thighed bass in bone and skin like the clearing Baby Suggs made for us Flesh of our Flesh Blood of our Blood Hair Teeth Nail Root Shell like this drum cut from the Coast shipped to here like this y'all like that *truly truly* like this . . .

Funeral Mass: Man 1

He says he'd like to say this: this is like the end of an era. Your father certainly was a dear, dear friend of mine, he says. And we all sometimes make turns in the road, and if your father made any turns in the road that might have affected anyone I pray that God will forgive him, and his family forgive him, but, he says, he'd just like to say now: So long for now, until we meet again, may God grant you safe passage, may God receive your soul.

The Industrious American Negro

"Whatever else the American negro
is, he is an American in spirit and
ideals. We have here the best peasant
labor in the world. It was trained in
a school that was probably one of the
most efficient in the world, the school of
slavery. The North cannot reach its mil-
lions of foreigners because of the bar-
rier of language, but there is no such
barrier here in the problem which con-
fronts us. The basis of religion is
....

"To the industrious negro, the white
man is a friend—I speak particularly of
the Southern white man who has, and
always will be our best friend. Get rid
of the vicious drinking, gambling, dan-
gerous nomads, if you have them, get
rid of them at any cost. They but draw
us down; have, and maintain in your
pursuits of labor and pleasure high
moral standards and your white neigh-
bor will not only respect but aid you.
All forms of labor are honorable, and
all forms of idleness are degrading."

"Evangelizing of Negro is Present Need, Says Divine: Bishop Thirkield Discusses Black Race before Baton Rouge Conference," *Times-Picayune*, April 14, 1915.

"Go Back to Soil is Message to Negro: Booker Washington Discusses Economic Problems Confronting Race in South," *Times-Picayune*, April 14, 1915.

Conversation in Bop #2:

To Miss New Orleans

We have always been here.

—Chitimacha Oral History

This is a Black school.

—James Hollins, 2015

Man, when you got to ask what is it, you'll never get to know.

—Louis Armstrong, 1949

Your high school's gone. 1201 S. Roman. Did you see me outside the chain-link, pricker
bushes overcoming concrete slabs whose brick halls you walked with ghost of Booker T.,
outside the auditorium where King of Zulus played in 1949, your commencement year,
years after Little Louis picked for food in this same Silver City dump, poisoned parcel
of plantation once Chitimacha land, me scavenging in tagged remains—Katrina Was
Here—skin for fractured floating bones, tired, did you? How much is too much?

Do you know what it means?

Like the day you taught me to spell "a lot": Daddy, is this right?
You showed me, but it looked wrong, the lonely "a," dejected "lot,"
each word a cell. You sure, I said. You laughed, like why would you
lead me astray, always pushing school like it'd make us free. *See?*
You showed me: pushed together the word was nothing but a misspelling
of something real, which I don't remember you explaining, but after,
alone and writing, still suspicious of the gaping space in this English,
I remember that. Of all moments, why this flimsy flesh of memory?

Do you know what it means?

The day the Wizard of Tuskeegee rolled into New Orleans the paper quoted the Assistant
Surgeon General: the Vieux Carré would be *one of the most rat-proof cities in the world.*
1915. Birth of a Nation, Burning Cross, Over 50 Lynchings, The Wizard's Death Year.

Go back to the soil, he said. You think he saw the steaming ulcer, the putrescence that would become your high school, first one built for Black kids, with no environmental remediation, & on the condition vocations for Negroes didn't compete with White folks?

Do you know what it means?

To dedicate or distribute or a portion of land or many as one, as in four trees once marked the boundary of the Chitimacha, the only Louisiana tribe to possess a portion of their aboriginal home—Watch their Isle wash away, or I might say to a child if you see a sign saying *Land & Negroes for Sale* we could be talking two types of lots or two types of Negroes, but, I'd add, that's another lesson. Whatchu you think Booker T. would say?

Do you know what it means?

Upon information and belief you inhaled toxic metals for four years. Liver, lungs, stomach, skin, blood, spleen, pancreas, damage to fetus, to brain, reproductive systems, to liver and kidneys, skin, eyes, nose, and throat. Upon information and belief extent of hazardous waste unknown.

Do you know what it means?

Is the lesson when things look/feel wrong they can still be right, like how they're rebuilding your school, replacing 6 feet of soil though contaminants go down for 15 feet or more, or is it this small sampling of you is one of the few I possess, and how they'll still want me to excavate your whole body, peel the membrane so they might pass to your fugitive life. I know, I know. You don't have to tell me. The story's in the subsidence.

Do you know what it means?

You never marched in the 50's or 60's, said you didn't wanna get your ass beat. So real it makes me laugh. Was that you saying back away at the bridge in Standing Rock, my clothes frozen from the glee of cops' waterhoses? Never thought I'd see you in that exhausted Negro Booker T. Only evidence of your revolts at work in the debris you carried home. If you're unhappy in your job you should leave, I said that sit down day. How old was I? You looked at me like I'd lost my last and only mind: *You think you're gonna be able to leave a good job just because you don't like it?*

Do you know what it means?

Recovery began this past December, the day before your five years. I wasn't there, I watched. Folks seem happy. It's good, who knows? Did you hear the children's brass, see the boy kick up dust, his feet a joyful crossing, a Legba incantation against antimony, barium, cadmium, copper, lead and mercury and zinc, second-lining his way like we been doing, no matter our lot, as our lot will do, over this pernicious unsettled ground.

Do you know what it means?

Do you know what it means?

To Get to the Cemetery

for Cynthia Marie Graham Hurd, Susie Jackson, Ethel Lee Lance,
Depayne Middleton-Doctor, Clementa C. Pinckney, Tywanza Sanders,
Daniel Simmons, Sharonda Coleman-Singleton, Myra Thompson,
and for the survivors

I.

Turn right at Las Cruces. The Dead End sign will take you to Paris Rose,
alive for seventeen years now she is a blue-stoned ruddy clay heart
almost four feet tall propped on wooden beams *Beloved daughter sister*
and friend Waiting for us on the other end a sad dream net hanging
from a wooden cross dead roses turned the dark of old scabs Fresh Flower
Food unopened rusted metal faces smiling stuck inside the ground.
She's nothing at all. She is something to someone you will never know.

II.

The first time you saw the flat marker of your father's death, a sterile strip
    of gauze in a field surrounded. Occasionally, flowers.

You remembered the stiff slow dance of two boy soldiers, their hard folding of
    the flag into your mother's open hands. Wailing Taps. *Whose life is this?*

Pour bourbon, cheers, salud, for the ones no longer here. Drink the rest. You left
    some coins, wore white that day—a baptism, a bride, a shroud—you, you—

You don't want to think anymore about the meaning of these things, one year to the
    day since you stood in the river where Tubman freed enslaved hearts.

You swore. Release what you no longer need: silence, fear, also shame. Listen:
    Whatever you do just stay away from the Bucket of Blood—

Your father's warning one Mardi Gras about a place from his youth that may
    or may not have existed in this one time of his telling.

But that day in the Quarter it was now always now his yesterday. Your
father knew time, how it could trick a man into forgetting—

Leave him sitting in a wheelchair in his own piss, wondering how he got
there, wondering if he was ever going to get clean again.

III.

Your dad, said the Chicano man at his wake,
your dad, said the man, I want you to know,
you kids should know your dad was a fighter.
Your dad, he didn't look like he could throw
down but he threw down if needed. Your dad
fought for us at work, fought for us long ago.

Your dad made sure there was a place for us
when there weren't a lot of us, and still—
there aren't, not enough, but your dad,
I have to say what he had to deal
with it took a toll, all that bullshit, ex-
cuse me, all that bullshit they made him feel.

All that bullshit, excuse me, from bosses,
all that bullshit in which he was caught
and he was smarter than all of them.
That bullshit, I mean racism, was a lot.
I mean your dad, man, was courageous,
Threw down when needed, always, always fought.

When I saw his name in the office newsletter
I had to come tell you. You kids should know:
Yor dad was a fighter. For us,your dad fought.

IV.

For seconds feel the cold that must come with dirt and dark. In this stalking
it's never been clear if it's been you or death. *What kind of person is
a slave to bones?* It will happen soon. For three seconds or more know this.

Say you are imagining things. Say you're being silly. Stop it. *You are living, you are alive, you are here,* words you say every morning since they removed the small butterfly of cancer buried deep in your throat.

Remember the pueblo a few days ago, the women dancing in two lines, their flowered dresses and pink flowers, their song. Remember the men dancing with them, the drummers, the rattle, the song like old school hip hop, like nothing else, its own thing inside its own thing and the man who asked if you were happy you waited through rain and mud: Yes. And what did you think of the dance, what of the dancers? Beautiful, but I don't know what I'm seeing, and you didn't know if your seeing was watching, if your watching was taking, if it was any different than the long line of watchers and takers that came before you, but you wanted to say in your seeing, watching, and being you felt something close to joy, as much joy as any Black person might feel in an occupied country. How—

He told you of other dances for young and old, each dance part of the seasons. See, this is where we dry the corn and up there's where we store it and what brings you here and where you from? he says. You say, My fa-her, New Orleans, Segregation, L.A., how you're writing Terror and Plantations, Love and Resistance. History and Memory. You feel like you're saying too much or too little or not enough of what's true so you stop. He says: you know the U.S. bombed the old church, one hundred fifty dead, and my father who used to be governor found a cannonball in the graveyard once when they were digging, rolled right up to his feet like it was yesterday—talk about your Indian antiqui-ties, and you both laugh because you know a good story when you hear one.

Because you know a good story can hold a hundred little lies and still bear the one truth we need. Because any storyteller worh their weight knows exactly what story to share in any given moment, and what's your name, he says, and I guess I'll see you around and he leaves you with the rolling cannonball and the ways the dead refuse our capture, and the dangers of walking over the dead without ceremony.

Later, your friend will laugh when you share the story. You tourists, he'll say, you'll believe anything we tell you. But stories, you'll say, stories. He'll shake

his head, disappointed at how easy it was for you to fall for
the earth releasing hundred-year old cannonballs. Listen, he'll say, no-
body really knows what's buried there. So it might be true then? You're not
listening. Why do you need to so badly believe this story's true?

V.

A few minutes earlier you sat in the new old church waiting for
the rain to stop, a covered coffin draped in summer pink to your right.
Later you learn the coffin is normal. You'll find them throughout the state.
You sat with lit candles in sand, painted yellow corn, squash blossoms and
beans, Saint Jerome, Kateri, the Virgin Mary, over one hundred fif-
ty people dead. You sat with layers of murder and belief and stumbled
to remember childhood prayers but there they were, faces thin and wanting—

Our father, I'm tired of grieving endless grief
    when a simple walk turns into communion with ghosts
    when a neighborhood park is named for a White murderer, enforcer of genocide—
        Hero Scout Citizen, He Led the Way—
            whose decaying body lies where Brown kids play baseball
and the other day two Black men and a Black boy raped and set a Black girl on
    fire
and before that the White cop's knees on the back of a fourteen-year-old Black girl crying
    for her mother
and a Black boy we murdered we say killed himself
and you're no longer nor will you ever be citizens
and today, again today, a White terrorist shot nine Black people in a Black church

    nine Black people in a Black church
    nine Black people in a Black church
    nine Black people in a Black church
    nine Black people in a Black church
    nine Black people in a Black church
    nine Black people in a Black church
    nine Black people in a Black church
    nine Black people in a Black church

say their names every one:

and a Black president sings this is about guns and this is about grace but
nothing about the amazing un-naming of what's killing us while
a grandmother tells a bloodied Black girl to play dead to live.
How many times have we played dead to live?
Where is our sanctuary? Where is our rest?
The dead say nothing.
Better people than you were powerless.
You are living, you are alive, you are here.

VI.

Take this small wing of windmill glinting through dust at your feet, stick it in
Your hair, walk among whirring stones, be your own *boisterous Black Angel*,
promise to return to this place where high desert sun makes absence in
windchimes ropes of shells photos fading fast, painted stones *forever in
our hearts*, and hundreds of unreal flowers look like the best houseparty
you never went to. Better this spirit flash than sterile strips of gauze.
It is this time/that matters/it is this history/I care about

> Remember your father singing at the bottom of the stairs.
> Remember your father singing at the bottom of the stairs early Saturday mornings.
> Remember the women singing and dancing. Remember the men singing and dancing
>   among and with them. Remember the seasons.
> Remember your father sang and danced even when you covered your ears
>   your father sang and danced, stomped his feet, and bounced to a
>   New Orleans rhythm only he could hear. Somewhere still
>   your father sings and dances.
>   He was living
>   He was alive
>   He is here
>   His yesterday is always now.
>   He is jazz and oysters, the Lakers and Dodgers, and he sometimes
>   drank himself to sleep and wake.
> Remember he fought for us.
> Remember he's only one man we designated Black
>   who sometimes played dead
>   to live—

Tell the ruddy heart you'll never know, whose birthday was six days ago, who you later learn died driving home from the Gorge to get food for her father who sold things on the bridge, tell her. I am, you say, not too loud, I am. Look at you, still talking to the dead. The Taos Pueblo Mountains peak in the bloody sky. The windows at the edges of this graveyard always look in and out. Keep on. Whisper promises no one in her right mind would try to keep. Always remember where you stand. Even when the living remains become their own coffins, remember. Remember.

STEPHEN LOUIS LEE

Stephen Louis Lee was an early trapper
and fur trader working out of Taos, and was a
friend and business partner of Kit Carson, the
Bents, and Ceran St. Vrain. He had a house
next to Kit Carson's in Taos, and owned a
store and tavern on the southwest corner of
the Plaza. He was also a distiller of the famous
whiskey "Taos Lightning," and served as
sheriff of Taos County following the annex-
ation of New Mexico in 1846. Lee was killed on
the roof top of his store by insurgents during
the Taos Rebellion of 1847.

Postlude

You think the book is done, and then out of the blue and for Valentine's Day, your mother sends you a box filled with 99-cent store trinkets. Buried underneath is a file of your father's performance reviews when he worked at the IRS in the early seventies and eighties, when he was one of the few Black folks employed. Your mother's note: *Keeper of the flame. Your father's journey through the impenetrable ceiling. Thought you might like to hold onto this.* As you read through his reviews, you think about your own annual reviews and the genre and performance of performance reviews within interlocking crushing systems, what we silence and what we resist.

1978: Has excellent anticipation. I have observed him managing his operation with a basic thrust towards preventing the occurrence of problems rather than solving problems after they occur. This is obviously made possible by his ability to keep abreast of day-to-day activities so that he can spend his time managing the future rather than reacting to the past.

You think about what it means to manage what hasn't yet come to be, and what it means to continue reacting to what's supposed to be said and done. How nothing is ever done, how we live in and with rememory. How the dead continue to find ways to speak to us, guiding us toward possible futures, even after death.

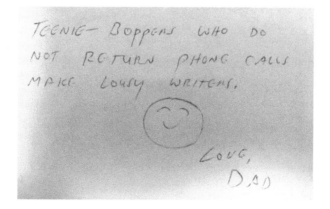

Give Thanks

To these lands and to the original caretakers of these lands; to every place I drove, walked, ran, wrote, and sometimes prayed; in recognition of stolen land, lives, and labor; and in recognition of our past and continued resistance;

To Daddy, your life and death guided and shaped this book, and continue to guide and shape past, present, and future stories; Mommy, your life guided and shaped this book, and continues to guide and shape past, present, and future stories; for the lives you both lived and are living, for the ways you continue to teach me to resist and love; to my brothers and sisters, always with me no matter how separated by distance; to my cousins, aunts, and uncles for providing lifelines to NOLA; and to my brilliant nieces and nephews who are mapping our past, present, and futures;

To the Black, Indigenous, and other women of color writers/thinkers/artists/ activists—living and dead, your loving work makes everything possible; so many to name, but a few that hovered close throughout the writing: Toni Morrison, Zora Neale Hurston, Barbara Christian, June Jordan, Luci Taphanoso, Leslie Marmon Silko, Audre Lorde, Ana Castillo, Dream Hampton, Gloria Anzaldua, Lucille Clifton, Angela Davis, Wendy Rose, The Combahee River Collective, Leanne Simpson, Saidiya Hartman, Harriet Tubman, and the creators of #BlackLivesMatter: Alicia Garza, Opal Tometi, Patrisse Cullors;

To every person I spoke with on my many trips across the country, to guides/ mentors/friends/fam: to Alexis Pauline Gumbs, for living queer Black brilliance and Black love, for creating space to remember Harriett Tubman, and for continuing to create Black Spaces for us rooted in the ways and words of Black womxn; to Carolyn Forché, for everything and for reading an early version of "The Forgetting Tree" with a close eye; to Tony Medina, for first introducing me to the bop form, for your poetry and activism—a perpetual North Star, you remind me we can and should do this work *not without laughter*; to Tracy K. Smith, for your kind listening and for suggesting I read a particular book when I was thinking about how to fill in silences; and to Kiese Laymon, a true brother, fam in the best possible way, whose "waves and waves of unreasonable black American love" hold me steady from afar;

To each anonymous reader who read the first draft of this book with clarity and attention, and who helped me see what I'd been unable to see; to Wayne State University Press and the women who created space for this book to come into being—Annie Martin, Kristina Stonehill, Rachel Ross, Kristin Harpster, Emily Nowak, Jamie Jones, and Polly Rosenwaike;

To colleagues at Michigan State University, which is on Anishinaabe lands: to Dylan Miner and Estrella Torrez, for all your art, stories, and for your longstanding loving commitments within and outside this so-called land grant institution; to Gordon Henry, for your friendship, support, and guidance; to Jeff Wray and Tama Hamilton-Wray for being here and making space for all of us, and to all Black faculty and students for holding it down in the face of persistent anti-Blackness; and to the many students in my creative writing workshops at MSU and elsewhere who have been a part of thinking deeply about creative writing and race and whose stories give me hope;

To Tamara Butler for inviting me to her class to share stories from this book when it was in its early form; to Briona Jones for being, and for the care you bring to all your work; and to Joy Priest for breathing Black poetry that lets us become more;

To the University of Washington, which sits on Coast Salish lands, and to its English Department, Creative Writing faculty, and other faculty who first heard the most complete version of "On Forgetting," and asked generative, loving questions that made me think more deeply about why and how;

To Margaret Burnham, founder of the Civil Rights and Restorative Justice Project at Northeastern University, for inviting me to share this work at the 6th Annual National Association of Community and Restorative Justice Conference on a panel about memory, the South, and resistance to terror;

To Taos Pueblo, to the 2017 Honorable Governor Ruben A. Romero and staff, and to Ilona Spruce, Tourism Director, for taking time to meet with me to consider "To Get to the Cemetery" to make sure I and the poem do as little harm as possible; for each thoughtful, loving comment made by everyone present, comments which remind me of the responsibility and care involved not only when writing but in how writing enters the world;

To Christopher Lujan, for encouraging me to think more critically about land, memory, and story; for speaking on my behalf with care, for the Pueblo Water

Protectors, for blue corn and chicos, for being a true caretaker of the land; and to Emileah Lujan, for your intelligence, fierceness, and love, and for the stories you're writing;

To my coven: co-conspirator, younger sis, daughter of the waters, digital and real-time orisha Jessica Marie Johnson, for continuing a long tradition of kitchen table conversations and asking me a question one morning you might not remember that I replayed as I wrote; and to my other coven-kin, co-conspirator, and faithful witness, Yomaira Figueroa, for creating space in your graduate course for me to share and remember the genesis of the "Ballad of Negro Judah," which helped me come to a decision about the final stanzas, and for working together to create space for women of color at MSU; and to Lisa Ze, for your rootedness in Black feminist ways of being that continue to inspire;

To Alyana Lee Eagle Shield and family—Red Rock, Kyyalyn, Waaruxti, and all, for Defenders of the Water School, for being and becoming a sister; and to Mel Martinez, Halle, and Little Mel, for warm coats offered after freezing water; for created relatives: To A. for telling me so many years ago to think carefully about Gorée Island and what it meant to be there in that place at that time;

To Richard Alonzo, there through everything; to Robert Soza, for needed loving reminders; and to Trish Hicks always;

To all in the Paris, Campbell, Lovell, Fisher, Riles, Barber, and Sokol families, and all our connected names, for extending family in ways I could've never imagined;

And to Django, there for every step, every breath, each step/breath made possible from the certainty of knowing you're present during and at the end of each journey, *Ever living; Ever loving;*

Finally, once again to the Honorable Governor Ruben Romero and staff for reminding me of the ways responses to this book might reverberate in ways I'm not able to anticipate; while I share everything in here with the best intentions, good intentions don't always mean a good end result; and so my sincerest apologies in advance if there's anything within or if there are omissions that do any harm.

Notes

iii: "Rememory." See *Beloved* by Toni Morrison.

vi: "To recall you all / demands the voice and memory / of brief madness beyond pain." See "To Those Gone Ahead" by Kofi Awoonor.

vi: "But it's freedom or death, exert speed till my last breath." See "U for Me" by Brand Nubian.

1: "we are the bones / of what you forget." See "To Make History" by Wendy Rose.

3: On Forgetting. The title of this essay is in conversation with Carolyn Forché's important work *Against Forgetting Twentieth-Century Poetry of Witness*.

4: "This is not a story to pass on." See *Beloved* by Toni Morrison.

7: Nottoway (Nottoway Plantation and Resort). See nottoway.com.

7: "Were probably well treated" and "It is difficult to accurately assess the treatment of Randolph's slaves." In 2013, Ani DiFranco tried to hold a "righteous" retreat at Nottoway and gave a first whack apology in which she admits she couldn't have conceived that holding any event on a plantation, especially a so-called righteous one, would "result in so much high velocity bitterness," the description she uses to describe the necessary critiques by Black women and others. (See "Ani DiFranco's Faux-pology: White Privilege and the Year in Race" by Brittney Cooper in *Salon*, and "Outrage Over Ani DiFranco's Planned Retreat at a Former Slave Plantation Isn't Just the Internet Overreacting" by Mikki Kendall in *The Guardian*.) While the plantation corrected their description of the treatment of enslaved people at Nottoway, their original description is preserved on other sites that critiqued DiFranco's so-called "righteous retreat." (See "Ani DiFranco, I am Disappoint" by Professor Pink in *Jezebel*). Also see Ani DiFranco's apology (Ani DiFranco, December 29, 2013, www.facebook.com/anidifranco/posts/10153706874455226).

8: "days of glory." See "Ani DiFranco, Slavery and the Subsidy of History" by Nathan Goodman in *Counterpunch*, www.counterpunch.org/2014/01/03/ani-difranco-slavery-and-the-subsidy-of-history/.

8: "Murder Mystery Dinner Theater." See Nottoway Plantation and Resort, http://www.nottoway.com/html/nottoway-murder-mystery-dinner-theater.htm.

8: "Honors all slaves buried throughout the United States and those slaves in particular who lie beneath the ground of Tremé in unmarked, unknown graves." See "St. Augustine Catholic Church of New Orleans," www.staugustinecatholicchurch-neworleans.org/hist-slave.htm

11: Vernon Dahmer, Clyde Kennard, John Frazier. https://wn.com/vernon_dahmer.

12: "Something we can't get over." See "Vernon Dahmer," http://wn.com/vernon_dahmer.

12: I'm thankful for a recent conversation in which someone from the Mississippi Band of Choctaw Indians reminded me Neshoba County occupies Choctaw Land. I'm thankful for a recent conversation in which someone from the Mississippi Band of Choctaw Indians reminded me Neshoba County occupies Choctaw Land. As this person shared with me, and as several other sources note, someone from the Choctaw community found the burned car of Schwerner, Chaney, and Goodman in Bok Cito Swamp, which is on Choctaw lands. I'm grateful for the way the person I was in conversation with also pointed out to me that the deliberate dumping of this car, and the dumping of murdered Black bodies on Choctaw lands during this time period, further communicated the complete disregard for Black and Native lives.

13: Several readings were helpful in learning about Clyde Kennard: "The Saddest Story of the Whole Movement: The Clyde Kennard Case and the Search for Racial Reconciliation in Mississippi, 1955–2007" by Timothy J. Minchin and John A. Salmond, www.mdah.ms.gov/new/wp-content/uploads/2013/07/kennard. pdf.; "Letter to the Editor from Clyde Kennard." See *Teaching a People's History: Zinn Education Project*, https://zinnedproject.org/materials/kennard-clyde/letter-to-the-editor-1959/; "Kennard, Clyde." *Teaching a People's History: Zinn Education Project*, https://zinnedproject.org/materials/kennard-clyde/; "Clyde Kennard: A Little-Known Civil Rights Pioneer" by Timothy J. Minchin and John A. Salmond, *Mississippi History Now: An Online Publication of the Mississippi Historical Society*, www.mshistorynow.mdah.ms.gov/articles/349/clyde-kennard-a-little-known-civil-rights-pioneer.

13–14: "Somehow I feel a great sympathy" and "We believe that for men to work together best." See "Letter to the Editor by Clyde Kennard, 1958," *Teaching a People's History: Zinn Education Project*, http://zinnedproject.org/materials/kennard-clyde/letter-to-the-editor-1958/.

14: "I have done all that is within my power." Letter to the Editor by Clyde Kennard, 1960." Ibid. http://zinnedproject.org/materials/kennard-clyde/letter-to-the-editor-1960/.

14: "Ode to the Death Angel" by Clyde Kennard, Wikipedia, https://en.wikipedia.org/wiki/Clyde_Kennard.

15: "Student Printz (March 20, 1964)." Special Collections, McCain Library and Archives, The University of Southern Mississippi, www.lib.usm.edu/spcol/exhibitions/item_of_the_month/iom_dec_07.html.

18: "We're the ranch hands and cowboys who opened up the West." "Remarks by the President at the 50th Anniversary of the Selma to Montgomery Marches," www.whitehouse.gov/the-press-office/2015/03/07/remarks-president-50th-anniversary-selma-montgomery-marches.

20: "I still shake. I still jump when I hear loud sounds." "Every day I think about it, just looking in the mirror and seeing the scars on my face. I'm reminded of it every day."

See "Long Forgotten, 16th Street Baptist Church Bombing Survivor Speaks Out" by Tanya Ott, NPR, www.npr.org/2013/01/25/170279226/long-forgotten-16th-street-baptist-church-bombing-survivor-speaks-out.

21: "When you think about that visit to Manzanar," These readings were helpful in considering the history of this area: "Concentration Camp" or "Relocation Center"—What's in a Name?" by James A. Hirabayashi, www.discovernikkei.org/en/journal/2008/4/24/enduring-communities/; Power of Words Handbook, https://jacl.org/wordpress/wp-content/uploads/2015/08/Power-of-Words-Rev.-Term.-Handbook.pdf, https://jacl.org/education/power-of-words/; "Paiute," *Virtual Museum Exhibit: Manzanar Historic Site,* www.nps.gov/museum/exhibits/manz/pre_war_manzanar.html; "DWP Archaeologists Uncover Grim Chapter in Owens Valley History," http://articles.latimes.com/2013/jun/02/local/la-me-massacre-site-20130603; "Manzanar," https://en.wikipedia.org/wiki/Manzanar#cite_note-Hirabayashi-19.

23: "by one of the first families to settle the Knoxville area." See "History of Ramsey House," *Historic Ramsey House,* www.ramseyhouse.org/about/history/.

24: "Boys hanging from the most beautiful sycamores in the world." See *Beloved* by Toni Morrison.

40: Harriet Tubman. In January 2017, the properties on the grounds became the Harriet Tubman National Historic Park. Information on donating to the Auburn site: www.harriethouse.org/membership.pdf.

43: New Town. For more on the wonderful work that has been occurring in the past several years and for more history of New Town: See http://newtownblacksburg.com/, www.blacksburg.gov/community/arts-and-culture/blacksburg-museum-and-cultural-foundation/st-luke-and-odd-fellows-hall, www.icat.vt.edu/grant/project/new-town-project.

43: "overlooking what used to be plantation land, overlooking and standing on what I later learn are lands of the Tutelo/Monacan Nation." See Monacan Indian Nation, www.monacannation.com/our-history.html; See "Virginia Tech to Hold First Pow Wow April 1" https://vtnews.vt.edu/articles/2017/03/inclusive-powwow.html; See "Trail Exposes Hidden History of Va. Indians," www.washingtonpost.com/wp-dyn/content/article/2007/06/22/AR2007062202003.html.

44: "she put me in touch with Ms. Beatrice Freeman Walker who grew up in New Town." See "Beatrice Freeman Walker Oral History Interview," https://vtechworks.lib.vt.edu/handle/10919/24714; https://vtechworks.lib.vt.edu/ "Beatrice Freeman Walker Video Interview," https://vtspecialcollections.wordpress.com/2014/01/23/beatrice-freeman-walker-video-interview/.

45: The image of the New Town map is a personal photograph of a detail of a map, which was shown to me by Lori, the then curator of St. Luke and Odd Fellows Hall. I owe so many thanks to Lori for her assistance. The map is in Martha

Shupp Phillips' thesis, *A Negro Neighborhood for Blacksburg, Virginia*, 1948, which is in Special Collections at Virginia Tech, http://addison.vt.edu/record=b1765567~S5.

48: "One Bright Morning / I'll Fly Away." See "I'll Fly Away" by Albert E. Brumley.

50: "Divided Heart: Part I." For italicized lines, see d. j. waldie, *Holy Land: A Suburban Memoir*.

53: "Who would believe / dead things could stumble back/and kill us." See "the news" by Lucille Clifton.

66: "She is listed in the Maryland Archive as the first Maryland woman who was reported to have resisted slavery," and she "may be the youngest woman ever to be executed in the United States." See Askia Muhammad, "Plantation Where 14-Year-Old Slave was Hung to Become Outlet Mall," www.newyorkbeacon.net/files/be1906s_1_.pdf; same article easier to read: www.finalcall.com/artman/publish/National_News_2/article_8591.shtml

71: The image from the Rough Minutes from Negro Judah's court case is used with permission from the Maryland State Archives. This image may also be found online at http://msa.maryland.gov/megafile/msa/speccol/sc5400/sc5496/010500/010538/images/mdsa_c1297_7.pdf; other sources were utilized to inform the writing of this poem. Some of the language in the poem is taken from a couple of newspapers that reported on this. I'm including just a few links here. See Salubria Plantation Tragedy, www.youtube.com/watch?v=8Xq9GFtrlbQ; Using Painful Pieces of History, Prince George's Hopes to Boost Tourism," www.washingtonpost.com/local/using-painful-pieces-of-history-prince-georges-hopes-to-boost-tour-ism/2014/06/03/525873c4-eb51-11e3-9f5c-9075d5508f0a_story.html; Salubria, www.mncppcapps.org/planning/bayne_july_27_2011_v1.pdf.; John H. Bayne, http://msa.maryland.gov/megafile/msa/speccol/sc5400/sc5496/010500/010538/html/010538bio.html.

72: "The Hanging Tree." Found in "Runaway Slave Advertisements 1745–1775: A Selection," http://nationalhumanitiescenter.org/pds/maai/enslavement/text8/virgin-iarunawayads.pdf

77: "On behalf of the President of the United States." Personal collection, pamphlet of the United States Air Force, Blue Eagles Honor Guard, March ARB.

83: *Nothing remembers. Everything remembers.* See "daddy" by Lucille Clifton.

92: *Ready or Not.* See "Ready or Not" by The Fugees.

93: *Sometimes it Snows in April.* See "Sometimes It Snows in April" by Prince.

95: *I am black alive and looking back at you. See "Who Look at Me" by June Jordan*

98: "Survivor of many." Many thanks to the dear friend who offered this phrase to me and gave me permission to share it.

99: "I feel as if I'm time traveling." At the College Language Association's convening in New Orleans, Edwidge Danticat gave a keynote in which she talked about portals.

100: "Strangled: Letter to a Young Black Poet." All words in this poem are from D. A.'s Facebook post about the energy it takes to exist in predominantly White spaces, posted November 28, 2014. D. A. is the wonderful poet, Derrick Austin, who has a beautiful collection of poetry, *Trouble the Water* (BOA Editions, 2016).

100: "blackpoetsspeakout." Black Poets Speak Out, "began as a response to a conversation initiated by Amanda Johnston. Jericho Brown, Mahogany Browne, Jonterri Gadson, and Sherina Rodriguez-Sharpe responded to the call with ideas, suggestions, and various plans of action. What resulted was a hashtag video campaign house on a tumblr site featuring hundreds of videos from Black poets reading in response to the grand jury's decision on November 24 not to indict Darren Wilson, the police officer who murdered Mike Brown." For more on #blackpoetsspeakout See https://blackpoetsspeakout.tumblr.com/About.

101: #BlackLivesMatter. The "Open Letter of Love" first appeared on Black Space online, and so was able to link to Alicia Garza's essay on the history of #BlackLivesMatter, which describes the work of Alicia Graza, Opal Tometi, and Patrisse Cullors in the creation of BlackLivesMatter, and also the theft of queer Black women's work. For more, see "A Herstory of the #BlackLivesMatter Movement," http://blacklives-matter.com/herstory/. The "Open Letter" was pushed into the world by the work of many, particularly Django Paris and Jessica Marie Johnson. Thanks also to Tamura Lomax at *The Feminist Wire* and Alfredo Artiles at *Equity Alliance Blog*, and to those who signed and shared with students.

107: *The work protects.* See Toni Morrison in "The Radical Vision of Toni Morrison" by Rachel Kaadzi Ghansah

109: Dispatch: Dearborn Heights: *our liberation is a necessity not an adjunct to somebody else's, to be recognized as levelly human is enough, Shaming is one of the deepest tools of imperialist White capitalist patriarchy.* See *Combahee River Collective Statement*, "What we don't know: the name of her murderer. Theodore Wafer." When Wafer murdered Renisha McBride newspapers reporting the murder initially weren't identifying him by name, and instead referred to him as the "homeowner." *Who is Killing Us?* See Mrs. Sara Small in "Who is Killing Us?" by Terrion L. Williamson, www.thefeministwire.com/2012/01/who-is-killing-us/; *Flesh that needs to be loved,* See *Beloved* by Toni Morrison.

113: Swing Low Suite. The image after "On Being a Vine" of the person wearing the "Warrior" earrings, and the image right before "Swing Low Suite" of a person looking out at a river are photos taken in South Carolina when we traveled to commemorate Harriet Tubman's freeing of over 700 at the Combahee River. The photos are used with permission. The photo of the person in the "Warrior" earrings is the amazing Kifu Faruq, "an farmerpreneur, baker, traditional herbalist, and teacher." You may find more of Kifu's work at Herbal Everyday (www.facebook.com/pg/Herbal-Everyday-744113228967957/about/?tab=overview). The person looking out at the river is the incredible Rashida.

113: The Combahee River Collective. Before we arrived at the Penn Center on Port Royal Island in South Carolina, Alexis Pauline Gumbs sent us a podcast to listen to as we made our way. The podcast was a mixtape, a digital altar really, and like with all altars, Lex made meaning through layering, through her selection of sounds and through the ways she invited each of us to participate in this sound space not only by listening but by creating moments in between music and her reading of excerpts from the Combahee River Collective Statement, in which she asked us to reflect on the ideas in the Statement and how these ideas connected to our lives and the journey we'd chosen to make to South Carolina. Even after I had published "Swing Low Suite," I knew it wasn't complete. It was missing other voices. Included, with permission, are excerpts from the podcast, along with the Combahee River Collective Statement, along with other voices, including Harriet Tubman's.

113: "Welcome loved ones" / "What is something you wanna get free from as part of this journey?" / "And what is the community that you would risk everything for even your own transformation?" Personal communication of Cambahee River Podcase by Alexis Pauline Gumbs.

113: "Be quiet for the sake of being 'ladylike'/ "be quiet to be less objectionable in the eyes of white/if Black women were free, it would mean that everyone else would have to be free; the only people who care enough about us to work consistently for our liberation are us." See Combahee River Collective Statement.

114: "The underground rail." See "U for Me" by Brand Nubian.

114: "have memories within that came out of the material that went to make." See *Dust Tracks on a Road* by Zora Neale Hurston.

115: "All water has perfect memory." See "The Site of Memory" by Toni Morrison.

115: "Be the fairy-winged one / Flitting from rock to rock." When I wrote these lines I was thinking of Ai Elo, a young Black poet, one of the twenty-one of us who gathered together to remember Harriet Tubman's resistance at Combahee. I didn't know Ai Elo well. I met her when we gathered for that weekend in 2013 at the Penn Center. Toward the end of the weekend (on the last day, I think), I told Ai Elo I imagined her with wings, something about the way she moved and her overall spirit, which was filled with light. Ai Elo looked at me and told me she was one of those kids who used to wear fairy wings wherever they went. At the time of revising first proofs for this book, word came through social media that Ai Elo had taken her life into her own hands. You can see a video of Ai Elo that Katina Parker created, which is part of the Many Voices Project, www.youtube.com/watch?v=hctz1pa8U-Q. You can read the poem, "Lessons on Scatting Under the Influence" by Ai Elo here, http://cavecanempoets.org/fellow/elo-ai/; and a video of Ai Elo reading here, www.youtube.com/watch?v=YAsKd7D3pl8&list=PLCACA38B2CBC54FDE.

116: "Pairs like we never see" / "A young one hangin' on behind" / "One han' roun' her forehead to hold on" / "'tother han' diggin into the rice-pot" / "Eatin' with all its might" / "Hold of her dress two or three more" / "Down her back a bag with a pig in it." See *Scenes in the Life of Harriet Tubman* by Sarah Bradford.

123: You just can't fly on off and leave a body. See *Song of Solomon* by Toni Morrison.

127: The Tree of Return. *stop the love you save may be your own*, see "The Love You Save" by The Corporation; *ooo la la la*, see "Ooo La La La" by Teena Marie and Allen McGrier; see "Fu-Gee-La" by the Fugees; *Rock Rock Planet Rock* and *don't stop*, see "Planet Rock" by Soul Sonic Force; *Iko Iko* and *my grandma and your grandma*, see "Jock-a-mo" by James "Sugar Boy" Crawford and "Iko Iko" by The Dixie Cups; *there's nothing better than love*, see "There's Nothing Better than Love" performed by Luther Vandross and Gregory Hines; *truly truly in love with you girl*, see "Truly" by Lionel Richie; *bend down low* and *Let me tell you what I know*, see "Bend Down Low" by Bob Marley; *me myself and I*, see "Me, Myself, and I" performed by De La Soul; *don't forget what you got*, see "Every Ghetto, Every City" by Lauryn Hill and David Axelrod; *Mississippi goddam*, see "Mississippi Goddam" by Nina Simone.

132: The Industrious American Negro. I cut and pasted these images to form one image. These are excerpts from articles that appeared on the same day, on the same page, in the *Times-Picayune* in 1915, the year Booker T. Washington died. My father attended Booker T. Washington High School in New Orleans. I realized how little I actually knew about Washington, and so began reading about Washington's tour of Louisiana the year he died (along with his other earlier visits) and about the development of the high school, which was built on an old dump. My father's high school diploma is one of the things that was in the box my mother gave to me after his death.

133: "To Miss New Orleans" and "Do you know what it means?" See "Do you Know What It Means to Miss New Orleans?" by Eddie DeLange and Louis Alter.

133: "We have always been here." See "Tribal History," *Sovereign Nation of the Chitimacha*, www.chitimacha.gov/history-culture/tribal-history.

133: "This is a Black School." See "The Tearing Down of Booker T. Washington High School, New Orleans, LA," *Everyday Nola* with Dr. Brice Miller, www.youtube.com/watch?v=vKm_Lc0gLbA.

133: "Man, when you got to ask what is it, you'll never get to know." See "Louis the First," *Time Magazine*, 1949.

134: "One of the most rat-proof cities in the world." See "To Make Orleans Most Sanitary City in Country" in *The Times-Picayune*, 1915.

134: "Upon information and belief." See "Notice of Intent to File Suit Pursuant to the Resource Conservation and Recovery Act 42 U.S.C. § 6972(b)(1) for hazardous waste violations at the Booker T. Washington High School, AI No. 36659."

139: "when a neighborhood park is named for a White murderer, enforcer of genocide" See Kit Carson and Kit Carson Park in Taos, New Mexico and efforts to rename it.

139: "and the other day two Black men and a Black boy raped and set a Black girl on/ fire." See Arnesha Bowers, June 17, 2015.

139: "and before that the White cop's knees on the back of a fourteen-year-old Black girl crying / for her mother." See Dajerria Becton. Officer Eric Casebolt pinned her to the ground on June 5, 2015. In January 2017, Becton filed a 5 million federal lawsuit against Casebolt.

139: "and a Black boy we murdered we say killed himself" See Kalief Browder, June 6, 2015. On May 25, 2017, on what would have been Kalief Browder's twenty-fourth birthday, a street sign was named in his honor.

139: "and you're no longer nor will you ever be citizens" See the Dominican Republic and Haiti, June 17, 2015.

139: "and today, again today, a White terrorist shot nine Black people in a Black church." See Dylaan Roof. The massacre occurred on June 17, 2015.

140: "Better people than you were powerless." See "Return" by Carolyn Forché.

140: "Boisterous Black Angel." See "For Each of You" by Audre Lorde.

140: "It is this time / that matters / it is this history / I care about. See "On a New Year's Eve" by June Jordan.

143: "You think about what it means to manage what hasn't yet come to be, and what it means to continue reacting to what's supposed to be said and done." After I completed a first draft and revisions of this book, I begin reading Christina Sharpe's *In the Wake: On Blackness and Being*. Sharpe's work has been helpful in thinking about this writing.

CPSIA information can be obtained
at www.ICGtesting.com
Printed in the USA
BVOW11s0843210318

510837BV00014B/29/P

9 780814 344262